COLLINS LIVING HISTORY

EXPANSION, TRADE and INDUSTRY

Christopher Culpin

Series editor: Christopher Culpin

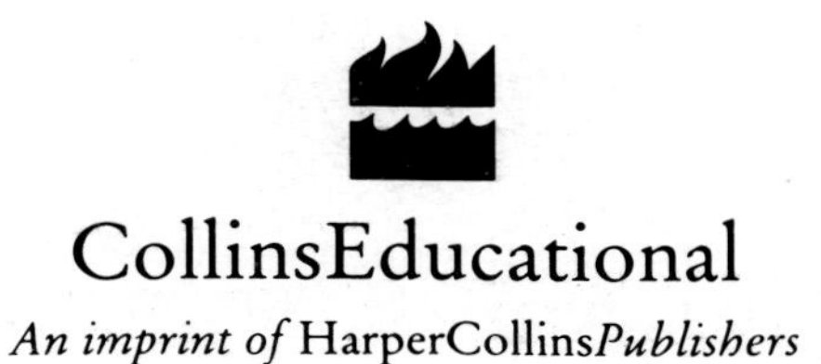

CollinsEducational
An imprint of HarperCollins*Publishers*

Contents

attainment target 1

Questions aimed at this attainment target find out how much you know and understand about the past. Some questions are about how things were different in history: not only people's food and clothes, but their beliefs too. Others are about how things change through history. They may change quickly but sometimes they change slowly, or only a little or sometimes the change is considerable. Other questions ask you to explain why things were different in the past, and why changes took place.

attainment target 2

This attainment target is about understanding what people say about the past. Historians, as well as many other people, try to describe what the past was like. Sometimes they say different things. This attainment target is about understanding these differences and why they occur.

attainment target 3

This attainment target is about historical sources and how we use them to find out about the past. Some questions are about the historical evidence we can get from sources. Others ask you about how valuable this evidence might be.

Introduction

The painting below by William Bell Scott (1811–1890) is called 'Newcastle Quayside, 1861'. It gives lots of evidence of what it was like in Newcastle at that time. In the centre, three brawny men hammer metal into shape. In the background, a steam train goes over the High Level Bridge over the River Tyne. All around are cranes, hooks, pulleys and metal castings. Bottom right is a working drawing of a steam locomotive. In the middle of the river is a 'keel-boat' (a coal-barge). Tied up at the quayside is a larger sailing ship. The little girl looks as if she is about to go on a long journey in it, perhaps emigrating from Britain. All is bustle, movement, noise and change.

This book is about change. During the 150 years it covers, industry and transport grew and Britain became a great trading nation. By the end, the British Empire was at its peak, and the lives of everyone in the country had been altered.

Town and country

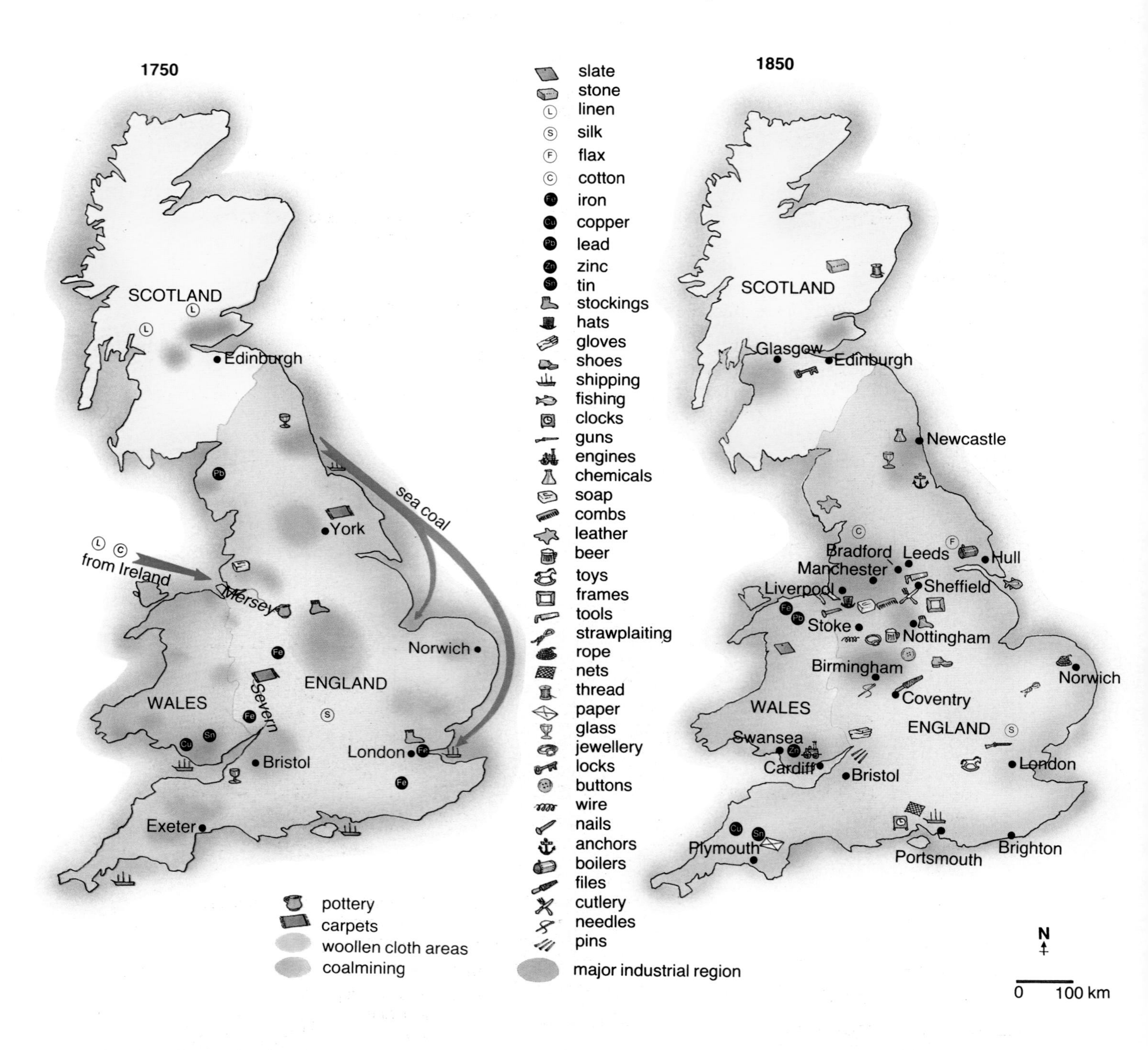

Maps showing the major cities and the main occupations of the workers. Despite the development of so many industries, the largest industry in 1850 was still agriculture.

The maps above show the largest towns in England, Scotland and Wales. You can see that there were many more large towns in 1850 and 1750. This was the result of people moving to find employment in the new factories.

By looking at the timeline opposite, you can discover some of the major events that occurred in Britain during the Industrial Revolution. You can trace how trade and industry expanded, and what reforms were attempted.

A.D. **TIMELINE**

1750

George II (1727–1760)

Bridgewater Canal opened 1761

Wedgwood's factory at Etruria opened 1769

Boulton & Watt begin to make steam engines 1775

Methodists leave C of E 1784

Palmer's mail coach, Bath to London 1784

George III (1760–1820)

1800

George IV (1820–1830)

Great Reform Act 1832

Factory Act 1833

Poor Law Amendment Act 1834

William IV (1830–1837)

First Chartist Petition 1839

1850

More people living in urban than rural areas 1851

Brunel's ship *Great Eastern* launched 1858

Victoria (1837–1901)

1900

1763 Britain gains colonies in Canada, the Caribbean and India

1771 Arkwright's factory at Cromford opened

1783 Cort's puddling furnace
US independence

1788 First colony in Australia

1792 French revolutionaries execute king

1811 Luddites in Nottinghamshire

1819 Peterloo

1830 Liverpool–Manchester railway opens

1866 Siemens' open-hearth process in steelmaking

1870 Education Act

1872 FA Cup starts

1875 Public Health Act
Artisans' Dwelling Act

1889 Great Dock Strike

1897 Queen Victoria's Diamond Jubilee

UNIT 1

First industrial nation

AIMS

This book deals with the years 1750 to 1900. In these years the British people were swept up in extraordinary changes because Britain was the first nation in the world to INDUSTRIALISE. In fact the changes were so great that they are often called an industrial REVOLUTION. In this unit, we will find out what this means and why it happened. Then we will look at how people's working lives were changed by industrialisation.

Think of the last time you went shopping. Wherever you live, the shops are full of large amounts of things for sale. Much the same things can be seen in shops all over the country. This is because Britain, and the countries which make most of the goods in our shops, are INDUSTRIALISED countries. They have INDUSTRIES which can make large quantities of goods and transport them over a wide area. It was not at all like this for the harvesters in Source 1.

In the mid 18th century, there were plenty of CRAFTSPEOPLE who made things to sell such as shoes, hats, gloves or clothes, but there were very few shops. These craftspeople worked in their own homes and sold their goods from there or from market stalls, like those in Source 2.

SOURCE 2
Norwich market in 1807.

SOURCE 1
'The Haymakers' by George Stubbs, a painting from the late 18th century.

From farm to factory

Despite the smart clothing the artist has given them, the people in Source 1 are farm labourers working at the hay harvest. Britain in 1750 was a land where most people lived in the countryside and farm work was the most common job. The industrialisation of Britain changed this in many ways. Most of all it changed people's jobs and so changed the place where they lived. For example, the workers in Source 3 worked in FACTORIES, the huge buildings behind them. They lived in an industrial town, Wigan in Lancashire.

Source 4 shows how industrialisation had begun to change shopping by 1900. It is a shop, not a market stall. It does not sell goods made by local craftspeople, but items made in factories. These items, such as Swan fountain pens, were advertised and sold all over Britain.

SOURCE 3
Factory girls in their lunch break, Wigan, Lancashire – a painting of the late 19th century.

SOURCE 4
A stationer's shop in about 1900.

Discuss these questions in pairs.

1. Describe the workers and workplaces shown in Sources 1 and 3.
2. What differences do you think there would be in the lives of the people shown in each source?
3. In what ways is shopping different in Sources 2 and 4?
4. What evidence of industry is there in Sources 3 and 4?

Were there any industries in Britain before 1750?

In the early 18th century, Britain was famous for what were known as 'manufactures', things made by hand. Hundreds of different items were made, from pins to furniture, but the most important was the making of woollen cloth. Everyone had to wear clothes, so plenty of cloth was needed. The main cloth-making areas were East Anglia, the West Country, Yorkshire and Lancashire.

There are several stages in the making of cloth. First the wool from the sheep is cleaned, then it is CARDED to make all the fibres run the same way. It is then spun into YARN on a **spinning wheel** and the yarn woven into cloth on a **loom**. The cloth might then be dyed, and dressed to make it smoother.

The domestic system

As Source 5 describes, many of these processes were done in people's homes. This is called the 'DOMESTIC SYSTEM'. Families often had a bit of land and a few animals but these did not take up all their time. Women collected raw wool, carded it, spun it (see Source 6) and passed it on to the WEAVERS. The men worked in the little workshops, weaving, dyeing or dressing the cloth. Quite young children were expected to help (see Source 7). Sometimes weaving was done at home too, usually by the men, and some houses were built with specially large windows to give more light for this job (see Source 8).

> There was not a beggar or an idle person to be seen because of their always being in business . . . This business is the clothing trade . . . Among the houses are scattered a number of cottages in which dwell the workmen, the women and children of whom are always busy CARDING, spinning etc . . . so that no hands being unemployed, all can gain their bread, from the youngest to the most ancient; hardly anything above four years old but its hands are sufficient.
>
> If we knocked at the door of any manufacturer, we saw a house full of lusty fellows, some at the dye-vat, some dressing the cloths, some at the loom, all hard at work.

SOURCE 5
Description of the area around Halifax, written by Daniel Defoe in 1724, in his *Tour through the Whole Island of Great Britain.*

SOURCE 6
Women working at home, spinning and winding yarn, 1814.

ACTIVITY

Divide the class in half. Work in pairs. Look at the sources and information on the domestic system. One half of the class finds as many reasons as possible why they think the domestic system was a good thing. Think about: family life, choice over working hours and speed of work, job satisfaction, anything else.

The other half finds as many reasons as possible why it was a bad thing. Think about: children working, health risks, dirt and pollution in the home, no control over quality of goods produced, anything else. Compare the findings of the whole class.

'Soon after I was able to walk I was employed in the cotton manufacture. The cotton was put in a deep brown pot with a strong mix of soap suds. My mother then tucked up my petticoats about my waist and put me in the tub to tread on the cotton at bottom. The dollops of cotton wool were then placed on the beams of the kitchen-loft to dry. My mother and grandmother carded the cotton by hand and it was then ready for spinning.'

SOURCE 7
From an account of the childhood of Samuel Crompton in the 1740s.

SOURCE 8
Weavers' cottages with large windows.

Other manufactures

Some places specialised in certain kinds of material. In the East Midlands 'framework knitters' made stockings and pieces of cloth for waistcoats. In Coventry workers made ribbons. In Lancashire they were beginning to make cloth from imported cotton or a cotton/linen mixture called 'fustian'.

In many parts of the country bricks were made by hand. Again, the whole family might help (see Source 9). The Midlands specialised in iron manufactures. Bars of iron were bought from forges and worked on in hundreds of little workshops. All sorts of items such as locks, chains and nails were made by hand in this way. In Sheffield the metal-workers turned out knives, scythes and scissors.

As Source 10 shows, farmwork was by far the most common job at the beginning of this period. But there were industries in Britain, and the number of people involved in them was by no means small.

SOURCE 9
Family making bricks by hand.

SOURCE 10
A modern historian's estimate of numbers of people in various jobs in the late 17th century.

Manufacturing	180,000
Mining	15,000
Building	77,000
Trade and commerce	135,000
TOTAL	407,000
Agriculture	1,500,000

Why did the cotton industry grow?

Source 11(a) shows the enormous growth of the cotton industry from almost nothing to a multi-million pound business. By 1850 over one third of a million people worked in it. Later in this unit we will see how other industries changed, but the description 'Industrial Revolution' seems to apply to cotton above all others. Why did it happen? There could be several reasons.

Idea 1: perhaps the rising British population all wanted to wear cotton clothes? Although the population was rising, as we shall see in unit 4, it was nothing like as fast as the growth of the cotton industry.

Idea 2: perhaps the cotton was sold abroad? Yes, most of it was. In 1850 over half of the value of all British exports came from cotton goods. This meant they had to be cheap. Look at Source 11(b); the price of cotton fell. So something happened which enabled cotton to be made in large quantities, much cheaper than before.

Idea 3: under the domestic system (see page 8) there was always a shortage of yarn for the weavers. It took up to 10 spinners to keep a weaver supplied with yarn. This was especially so after the invention, by John Kay in 1733, of the **flying shuttle** which enabled weavers to work even faster. Inventors put their minds to making new machines to spin more yarn.

a Value of cotton cloth sold		**b** Price of a length of cotton cloth	
1770	£600,000	1780	£2.00
1820	£18,500,000	1812	65p
1860	£33,000,000	1860	25p

SOURCE 11
Value and price of cotton sold.

'It was known that he had made a spinning machine and his wife boasted of having spun a pound of cotton during her short absence from the sick-bed of a neighbour. The minds of the ignorant and misguided multitude became alarmed and they broke into his house and destroyed his machine and part of his furniture.'

SOURCE 12
From a description of Hargreaves' invention, published in 1808.

SOURCE 13
A 96-spindle water-frame, from Arkwright's mill, now in Helmshore Museum, Lancashire.

Hargreaves' Spinning Jenny, 1764

Hargreaves' first machine could spin eight SPINDLES at once. Later versions could spin up to 80 spindles. It was worked by hand and spun a fine but weak thread. As Source 12 shows, the invention was not popular with spinners.

Arkwright's Frame, 1769 (see Source 13)

This invention produced a strong, coarse thread. Arkwright insisted that only large versions of it should be made, driven by horse- or water-power. Spinning now had to be done in factories. (You can read more about Richard Arkwright on pages 12–13.)

1. Read Source 12. How did the neighbours find out what the spinning jenny could do?
2. Why do you think they were so angry?
3. What does the writer of this source think about the angry neighbours?

Crompton's mule, 1779

This machine produced a strong, fine yarn. It too had to be powered by water or steam so was only used in factories. Mules with 400 spindles were soon being made; in 1825 a mule which could spin 2,000 spindles was built.

Cartwright's power loom, 1785

Weaving was so complicated that it seemed unlikely that it could ever be done by a powered machine. Cartwright's invention did not work well and it was not until the 1820s that successful power looms began to be used in factories. However, by 1860 there were 400,000 of them in use.

Factories

Most of the new inventions which transformed the cotton industry could only be used in factories. They were too large to be used in people's houses. Most of all, their huge increase in output came from using stronger power than human muscles could provide.

Factories already existed in the textile industry: Source 14 shows a silk factory in Derby. New industrialists like Richard Arkwright and Jedediah Strutt copied the idea: Source 15 shows Strutt's factory at Belper. The huge waterwheel which powered it all can be clearly seen. Later factories used steam-power. Source 16 shows how amazing the use of steam-power seemed to people at the time. (See pages 14–15 for more about water- and steam-power.) By 1850 there were nearly 2,000 cotton factories in Britain.

SOURCE 14
The Lombe brothers' silk mill at Derby, built about 1717.

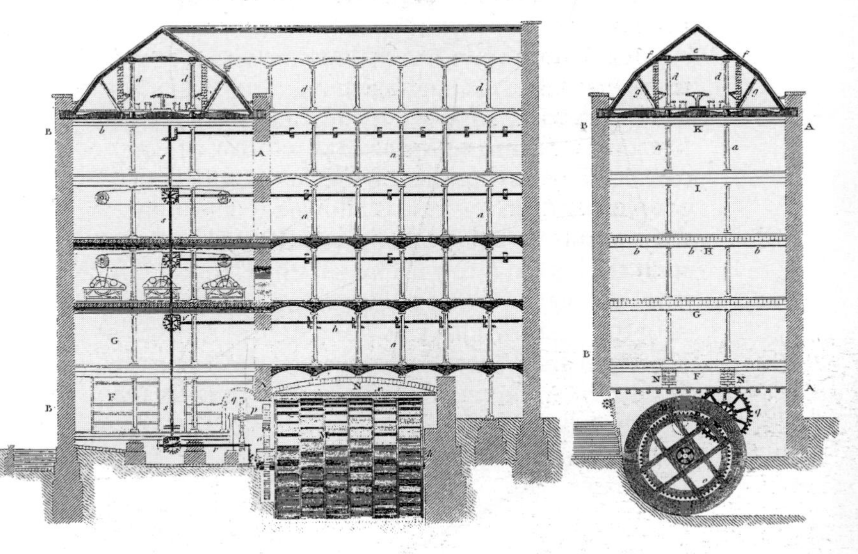

SOURCE 15
Diagram of Jedediah Strutt's cotton mill at Belper, Derbyshire, in 1819.

> A cotton-spinning factory offers a remarkable example of the use of very great power. Often we can see, in a single building, a steam engine set in motion 50,000 spindles. The whole factory requires but 750 workers. But the machines, with the assistance of that mighty power, can produce as much yarn as formerly could hardly have been spun by 200,000 men, so that each man can produce as much as formerly required 166! In 12 hours the factory produces 62,000 miles of thread, which would encircle the earth two and a half times!

SOURCE 16
From *History of the Cotton Manufacture in Great Britain*, by Edward Baines, published in 1835.

attainment target 1

1. How do the inventions described on these pages explain the figures in Source 11(a)?
2. What reasons were there for the fall in the price of cotton shown in Source 11(b)?
3. How do you think an invention like the frame in Source 13 would affect the lives of hand-spinners: after 6 months? After 5 years?
4. Which do you think was the most important cause of the rise of the factory system: all the new inventions? One of the new inventions? The need for power?
5. Explain how all these causes of the factory system are linked.

Arkwright – father of the Industrial Revolution?

The Victorian writer Thomas Carlyle was amazed by the life story of Richard Arkwright (Source 17). He wrote: 'Oh reader, what a historical phenomenon is that bag-cheeked, pot-bellied, much-inventing barber.' It is certainly a classic story of 'rags to riches'. When you have read these two pages you can make up your own mind about him. Was he a hero? A villain? A con man? A clever business man?

Richard Arkwright was born in 1732 in Preston, Lancashire, the youngest of 13 children. His family was poor and when he grew up he became a barber. Many people at that time wore wigs and he went into business buying people's hair and turning it into wigs. As he travelled round Lancashire from his home in Bolton he heard a lot about cotton MANUFACTURING. He realised that there was money to be made if someone could invent a machine to spin more yarn.

Soon he was spending all his time and money trying to make spinning machines. Eventually his wife, in disgust, smashed his models and left him. Arkwright **patented** his 'Frame' in 1769. (If you patent a new invention you register it with the government. No one else is allowed to use it unless they pay you money, called a **royalty**.) This 'Frame' spun the cotton into yarn by passing it through four pairs of rollers moving at increasing speeds. It is doubtful that the idea was Arkwright's. As early as 1738 Paul and Wyatt had suggested the roller method of spinning. John Highs then took up the idea, but did not complete the machine. The rest of the story is told, in its different versions, in Sources 18, 19 and 20.

SOURCE 17
Sir Richard Arkwright (1732–1792).

'After many years' intense and painful application I invented about the year 1768 the present method of spinning cotton built upon very different principles from any invention that had gone before it.'

SOURCE 18
Arkwright's own description of the invention of the 'Frame'.

In 1767 Arkwright fell in with Kay, a clockmaker at Warrington. Kay told him of Highs' scheme of spinning with rollers. Arkwright persuaded him to make a model of Highs' machine. He also persuaded Kay to work for him. There is no evidence to show that Arkwright had ever thought of making such a spinning machine before his interview with Kay at Warrington. Kay appears not to have been able to make the whole machine and therefore applied to Peter Atherton, an instrument maker, to make it.

SOURCE 19
Description of the invention of the 'Frame' by Edward Baines, an admirer of Arkwright, written in 1835.

'Mr Arkwright roundly asserts that he invented the frame round about 1768 . . . What effrontery! His abilities consisted solely in having cunning enough to pump a secret out of a silly, talkative clockmaker and having sense enough to know when he saw a good invention.'

SOURCE 20
Description of the invention of the 'Frame' by another historian of the cotton industry, Richard Guest, written in 1823.

Arkwright and factories

Arkwright insisted that the only versions of the 'frame' which could be made were large. They were too large for people's homes and required power to drive them. Anyone wanting to use a frame had to build a factory.

Building a factory cost a lot of money. We shall see throughout this book that new processes in industry often required CAPITAL, large sums of money. The people who put up this money are called CAPITALISTS. They expect that the business they INVEST in will make money for them in return.

Arkwright was not rich but went into business with John Smalley, Samuel Need and Jedediah Strutt. Their first factory, in Nottingham, was small and the frames were driven by horses. In 1771, Arkwright opened a large factory at Cromford, Derbyshire, powered by water (Source 21).

People who run a business, hoping to make a profit for themselves and for capitalists who have put money into the business, are called ENTREPRENEURS. Arkwright was a hard-working entrepreneur. His first factory employed 300 workers. Soon he was the owner of ten factories. He regularly worked from 5 a.m. to 9 p.m., travelling on relays of horses between his factories. In several places he built good houses in order to attract the many workers he needed (see Source 22). He built pubs and chapels for them and gave prizes to good workers. He also had very strict discipline in his factories. His workers, including children, worked very long hours.

Arkwright became a rich man. He lived in Willersley Castle, was made High Sheriff of Derbyshire in 1785, and was knighted in 1786. He died in 1792.

SOURCE 21
Arkwright's factory at Cromford, Derbyshire, painted by Joseph Wright of Derby (1734–1797).

SOURCE 22
Houses in North Street, Cromford, built by Arkwright.

attainment target 2

1 What truths, untruths and opinions can you find in Sources 18, 19 and 20?

2 What was Arkwright's contribution to:
  a new processes in the cotton industry?
  b the factory system?
  Use the sources to explain your answer in both cases.

3 'A great entrepreneur who showed that anyone can go from rags to riches.'
  'A cunning operator who rose to wealth and power on other people's ideas and money.'
  Which description do you think best fits Sir Richard Arkwright? Give reasons for your opinion.

What made the wheels go round?

For centuries the only forms of power for those who needed more than humans or animals could provide came from wind or water. Windmills gave only about 15 HORSE-POWER, and could only work irregularly. Waterwheels, however, were used in great numbers, all over Britain. The need for more power for factories and ironworks led to a marked improvement in waterwheel design. John Smeaton, at the Carron Ironworks in Scotland, made larger and more efficient wheels. Many early cotton factories found them quite good enough. (See Source 23 and also the huge wheel in Source 15 on page 11.)

The Cyfarthfa Ironworks in Wales used a wheel 50 feet (over 15m) in diameter. These giants could produce up to 200 horse-power, far more than any early steam-engine; the motion was steady and constant, unlike the jerky movement of steam-engines. Only after about 1850 did steam-power really overtake water-power.

SOURCE 23
Waterwheel at the cotton mill at Cromford, Derbyshire.

> I had two motives in offering you my assistance, which were love of you and love of a money-getting idea.
>
> I realised that your engine would require money, accurate workmanship and good selling to make the most of it. The best way of doing this was to keep it out of the hands of ordinary engineers who would be liable to produce inaccurate workmanship. My idea was to set up a factory near to my own by the side of our canal where I would erect all necessary for the completion of the engines and from which we would serve the world with engines.

SOURCE 24
Extract from a letter from Matthew Boulton to James Watt, 1769.

> 'Mr Wilkinson has improved the art of boring cylinders so that a 72-inch [1.8m] cylinder is no further from absolute accuracy than the thickness of a thin sixpence.'

SOURCE 25
Extract from a letter from James Watt to John Smeaton, 1776.

Steam-engines

Thomas Newcomen had invented a workable steam-engine back in 1712. It was enormous, slow and inefficient. IRONFOUNDERS could not make the cylinder accurately enough to prevent it leaking steam. It could only provide an up-and-down motion. The cylinder had to be continually heated and cooled, so it used huge quantities of coal. It was used to pump water out of coalmines but did not seem to have any use in factories.

In 1764 James Watt, a scientific instrument maker at Glasgow University, was asked to repair a model of a Newcomen engine. He saw that it would be improved if the steam could be drawn off into a separate cylinder, or condenser, and cooled there: the main cylinder would stay hot, the condenser would stay cool. He had no money of his own, so went into partnership with John Roebuck, of the Carron Ironworks. However, he could not get the cylinders made accurately enough.

Then Roebuck went broke and Watt teamed up with Matthew Boulton, who ran an ENGINEERING works in Birmingham. Boulton's motives for doing this are described in Source 24. Boulton was friendly with an ironmaster, John Wilkinson, who had a machine for boring accurate holes to make cannon. At last Watt could get his cylinders made accurately. He wrote enthusiastically to Smeaton about it (see Source 25) and Boulton and Watt began making engines in 1775. Further improvements turned the up-and-down motion into a round-and-round motion. The engines were now suitable for driving machines and removed the jerkiness (Source 26).

SOURCE 26
A Watt engine of 1788, in the Science Museum, London.

Steam-power in industry

Owners of ironworks, coalmines and Cornish tinmines took up Boulton and Watt's engine in a big way. The first all-steam cotton factory was started at Papplewick, Nottinghamshire, in 1785, but steam-power was generally slow to catch on in the cotton industry.

By about 1820 steam-engines were being more widely used to drive large new mules and power looms. The effects of this are described on page 11. They were also used for other processes in the cotton industry, such as printing patterns on cloth (Source 27). By 1851, seven out of eight cotton factories were powered by steam.

Steam-power also came late to the woollen industry of Yorkshire. When it did, huge mills were built for them, like the one described in Source 28.

Any industry requiring large amounts of power was using steam by 1850. Steam-engines were used for sawing wood and stone, pressing oilseed, grinding cutlery, rolling metal sheets or tubes, twisting ropes and drawing wire. They were used to pump water in mines, breweries, tanneries, soapworks and ironworks.

SOURCE 27
Steam-powered calico-printing machines, 1834.

'When the works are finished 4,500 hands will be required to keep them going. The weaving shed will contain 1,200 looms. The steam-engines to work them are equal to 1,250 horse-power.'

SOURCE 28
Description of the opening of Titus Salt's new woollen mill at Saltaire, near Bradford, from the *Illustrated London News*, of 1 October 1853.

Discuss these questions in pairs.

1. Read Source 24. What did Matthew Boulton and James Watt each contribute to the success of their partnership?
2. Why was there a delay between the invention of Watt's steam-engine and its widespread use? How long was this delay?
3. The machines in Source 27 replaced hand-printing. How would this change affect the skilled workers who used to do this job?

ACTIVITY

Factory-owner

You are a CLOTHIER in Lancashire. You have the money to buy large amounts of raw cotton at Liverpool docks. You send this around to be turned into cloth in the homes of the spinners and weavers and then sell the cloth.

1 You have seen the new spinning machines which have been invented. It is 1780. You decide to set up a spinning factory in the area where you live, shown on the map. You have five possible sites in mind: A, B, C, D and E.

There are three important things to think about:

i) The site must be beside a river or stream to drive the waterwheel.

ii) There must be good road links, so that you can get the raw cotton to your factory and transport the finished yarn to the weavers easily.

iii) It should be near a town or village so that you can easily get enough workers for the factory.

Use the table (right) to calculate which is the best site. Give each site a mark out of five for each of the three factors. Then choose the best site by adding up the total marks for each.

2 It is 1830. You are the son or daughter of the original owner and you have a new decision to make: where to put a new factory. This new factory will have both mules for spinning and power looms for weaving. It will be driven by a steam-engine. The three factors this time are:

i) Easy access to coal for the furnace of your steam-engine.

ii) Good transport links.

iii) Even more workers will be needed.

Use the table to calculate the best site in the same way as before.

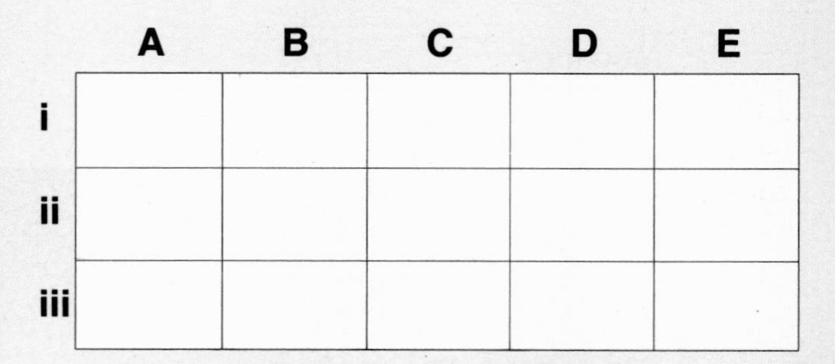

	A	B	C	D	E
i					
ii					
iii					

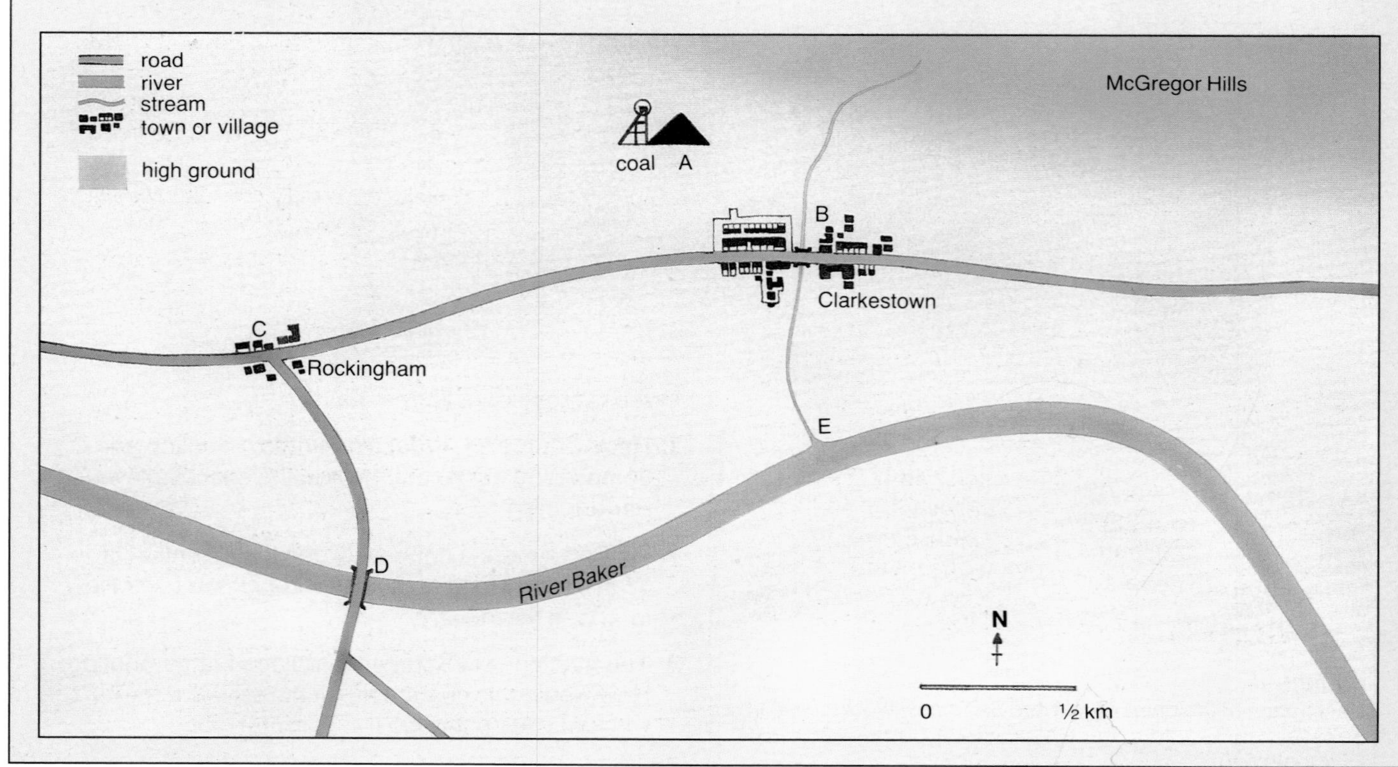

Why is Coalbrookdale so important?

The Industrial Revolution needed a new, strong material to work with. This material was iron, which soon replaced wood in making all kinds of industrial products, from ploughs to looms, from steamships to nails.

Iron is made by heating iron ore to high temperatures in a FURNACE with limestone, until it becomes molten. This is called SMELTING. The liquid iron can then be poured into moulds. This is **cast iron** and is strong but brittle. The early stages of the Industrial Revolution used lots of cast iron. The iron from the furnace can be re-heated and hammered in a FORGE to remove impurities. This is called **wrought iron** and is less brittle but softer than cast iron. **Steel** is made by heating iron to very high temperatures. It is pliable but strong.

Iron had been smelted in Sussex for centuries, mainly for use in making cannons. By the 18th century the industry was in difficulties. The main problem was the need for fuel to heat the furnaces. Coal could not be used because it contained impurities which spoiled the iron. CHARCOAL was used but it was in short supply: about an acre of woodland was needed to make the charcoal to smelt a ton of iron.

SOURCE 29
Painting of Coalbrookdale in 1777.

The Darbys of Coalbrookdale

In 1709 Abraham Darby set up an ironworks at Coalbrookdale, Shropshire. The site had iron ore, limestone and coal nearby and the River Severn provided good transport. Darby had worked in the MALT industry, which used coke for heat. He began to use COKE in his furnace and found that it worked. The Darby family were Quakers, pacifists, so he used his iron to make cooking pots, not guns.

Over the years the Darby family contributed to many of the new ideas of the early Industrial Revolution. They made boilers for steam-engines, opened up new furnaces and forges and linked them with cast-iron rails. One of Boulton and Watt's first steam-engines was bought for use at Coalbrookdale. Source 29 shows the area in 1777.

Abraham Darby III, grandson of the first Darby, had eight furnaces and seven forges by 1785. He looked for new uses for all the iron he could produce. The iron bridge (Source 30) was built to show that iron could be used in ways that people had not thought of before.

SOURCE 30
The iron bridge at Coalbrookdale, opened 1781.

What do Sources 29 and 30 tell us about the effects of the Industrial Revolution on the landscape?

The growth of iron and steel

Look at Source 31. Read Source 33. Compare them with Source 29 on page 17. What changes have taken place in the iron industry?

It has become a large-scale, heavy industry. In 1750 about 17,000 tons of iron per year were being made in Britain from about 50 furnaces; by 1827, 700,000 tons were being made per year, from 284 furnaces. Where was it all going?

The Industrial Revolution needed as much iron as the furnaces could produce. Wrought iron is purer than cast iron and much more useful, because it is not so brittle. But it seemed impossible to make wrought iron in large quantities because the iron was all mixed up with the coal or coke in the furnace. In 1783 Henry Cort discovered a new method of making wrought iron, called a 'puddling furnace'. The coal was kept separate from the iron, which was stirred, or 'puddled', until it was pure. The lumps of wrought iron were then taken out of the furnace and rolled while they were soft to make bars or sheets.

There was a huge demand for iron for railways, as well as for steam engines and ships. How did they make so much more?

Using the figures above for iron production for 1750 and 1827, work out on a calculator the average production from each furnace.

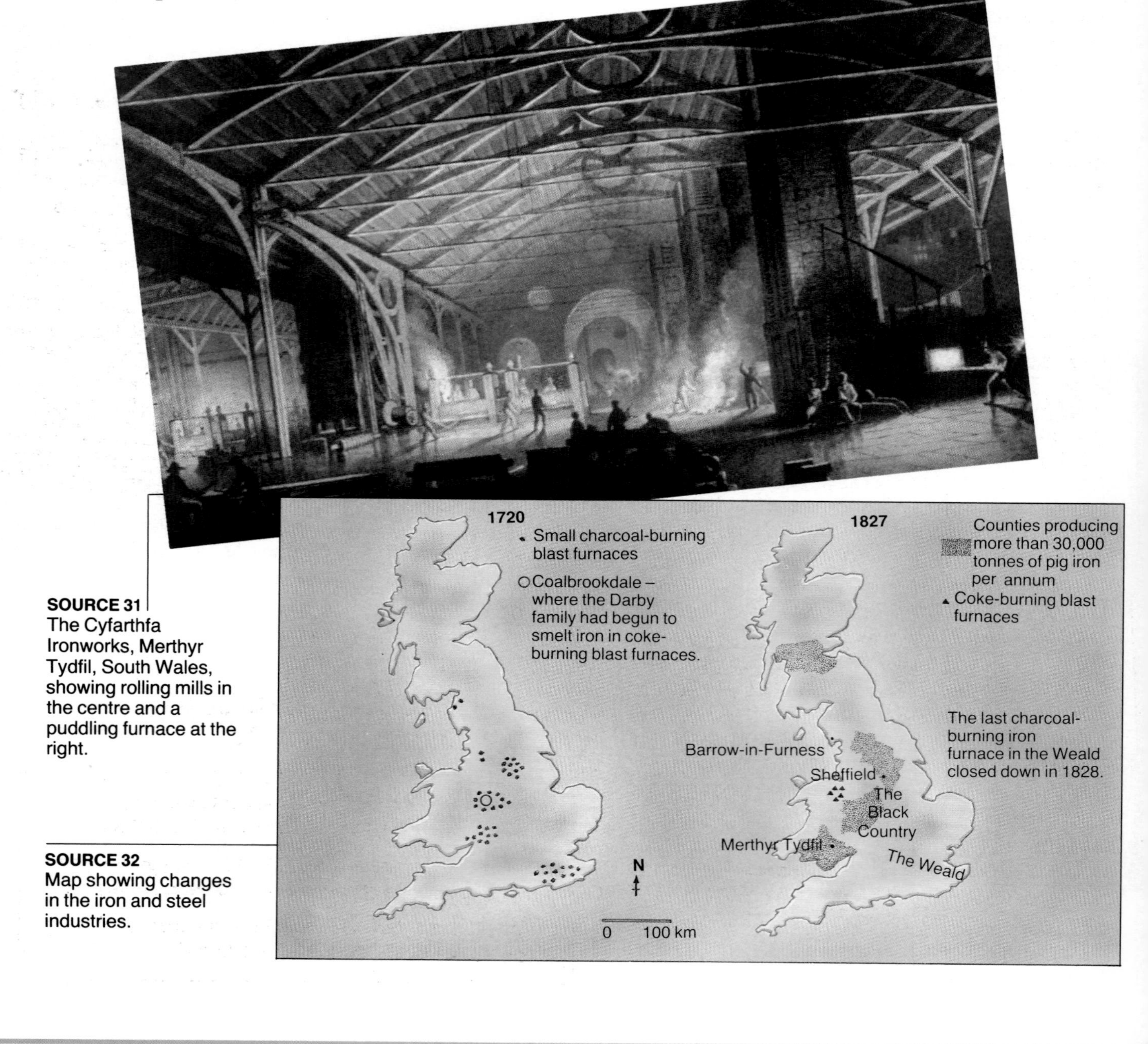

SOURCE 31
The Cyfarthfa Ironworks, Merthyr Tydfil, South Wales, showing rolling mills in the centre and a puddling furnace at the right.

SOURCE 32
Map showing changes in the iron and steel industries.

Obviously, one answer was bigger furnaces. Another answer was to combine BLAST FURNACES, forges and rolling mills on the same site: an **integrated ironworks**. It made sense to do this as the processes were linked and they could share the power of large steam-engines.

The biggest integrated ironworks in Britain was at Merthyr Tydfil in South Wales. There Richard Crawshay took up Cort's invention in a big way (see Source 31). John Guest did the same at his Dowlais works, also in Merthyr. By 1850 there were 47 furnaces in the town, employing 18,000 people.

It also made sense to build ironworks on or near coalfields as coal was the fuel for the furnaces and steam-engines. Other important ironmaking areas can be seen in Source 32. There were 160 furnaces in 50 integrated ironworks in the Black Country by 1850 (see Source 33).

Steel

Steel is even more useful than wrought iron as it is stronger. However, before 1850 only small amounts could be made, so it was very expensive.

Henry Bessemer's 'converter', invented in 1856, could make 20 times as much steel as before, in a quarter of the time. Unfortunately, it could not be used with certain kinds of iron ore. Siemens' 'open hearth' process, invented in 1866, was even cheaper than Bessemer's; the Gilchrist-Thomas process allowed most kinds of iron ore to be used. By 1900, nearly 5,000,000 tons of steel were being made per year in Britain. It was used in shipbuilding, railways, mining equipment, bridges and machines of all kinds (read Source 34). Much of this steel was made in integrated steelworks like the one described in Source 35.

> The Black Country is not pretty. The earth seems to have been born inside out. Nearly all the surface of the ground is covered with cinder heaps. By day and night the country is glowing with fire and the smoke of the ironworks hovers over it. There is a rumbling and clanking of iron forges and rolling mills. Workmen covered with smuts and with wild fierce white eyes are seen among the glowing iron and dull thud of the hammers.

SOURCE 33
Nasmyth, writing about the Black Country in the 1850s.

SOURCE 34
Advertisement for Sheffield steel products.

> 'The eleven large furnaces are capable of making iron at the rate of 500 tons a week each, at a price of £4 per ton. The steelworks will convert weekly about 1,000 tons of iron into steel, selling for £12 to £14 per ton.'

SOURCE 35
Description of the iron and steel works at Barrow-in-Furness, from the *Illustrated London News* of 19 October 1867.

1. What does Source 31 tell you about working conditions in the large ironworks in South Wales?
2. Compare Sources 29 and 33. What do they tell you about the scale of ironmaking at different dates?
3. What do they tell you about the effects of ironmaking on the environment at different dates?

Why was Josiah Wedgwood so successful?

Josiah Wedgwood was born in 1730. At the age of 9 he began work in his family's pottery. In 1759 he set up his first pottery with a capital of £20. When he died in 1795 he was worth £½ million. How did he achieve this?

Changes in public taste

In the early 18th century the drinking habits of the British people were changing. Instead of drinking ale out of leather, PEWTER or wooden mugs, people began to drink tea, coffee and chocolate. They began to need cups, saucers, teapots and milk jugs. British pottery at that time was dark, rough and heavy. In the 18th century people thought it was more refined to drink from crockery that was creamy, smooth, light and delicate. This was imported from China or France. English potters began to try to copy it. Thomas Whieldon was among the earliest potters to discover that a mixture of china clay from Cornwall, with ground-up flint, made a pottery that fitted the public's new taste. Wedgwood worked for Whieldon.

SOURCE 37
A bottle-kiln at a pottery museum.

> From the Lizard they returned by Redruth and Truro, looking for 'soap-rock' [china clay] all the way. On 10 June they found a farmer, a Mr Trethaway, who possessed a little estate and Mr Wedgwood agreed with him for a lease. The farmer said he would lease us the clay on the estate for so many years. He asked 20 guineas a year rent. Wedgwood offered ten. He accepted.

SOURCE 36
From Wedgwood's *Cornish Journey*, 1775.

Wedgwood's abilities

Wedgwood brought all kinds of other skills together in setting up his own business and making it prosper. For a start, he knew a great deal about making pottery. He invented new colours and new designs. He used ideas from Roman and Greek vases to decorate his pottery (see Source 39). Like many people in the 18th century he was interested in science, especially in the science of making, decorating and glazing pottery. He invented a thermometer for use in the pottery kiln. He bought shares in a china-clay mine in Cornwall in 1775 (see Source 36).

The factory system

Like many industries at that time, pottery was made in the domestic system, with lots of tiny family workshops and kilns (Source 37). All the different processes of preparing the clay, mixing, throwing the pots, firing, decorating, GLAZING etc. were done in different places. Wedgwood set up a factory where all these processes were carried on together. This meant that he could control the quality of work that his employees produced.

In 1769 he built a large new factory at Etruria with houses for the workers nearby. The belfry can be clearly seen in Source 38.

New technology

Wedgwood was alive to all the new ideas of his time. As Source 38 shows, the Etruria works were built by the Trent and Mersey Canal. Wedgwood could see the advantages of a canal and put some of his own money into building it. It ensured a steady supply of clay and a safe means of getting his pots to customers (see unit 3). He was also an early buyer of one of Watt's steam-engines for use in his factory.

SOURCE 38
Wedgwood's 'Etruria' factory beside the Trent and Mersey Canal.

SOURCE 39
Eighteenth century Wedgwood candlestick and vase.

Selling

Wedgwood was a good salesman, too. He knew what the public wanted and how to make it. Designs like those in Source 39 were popular. He had showrooms in London, Bath, Bristol and Dublin, where customers could see and order his wares (Source 40). He employed travelling salesmen. He used advertising and had catalogues printed. These were translated into other languages in order to sell in Europe. Special orders, such as a 950-piece dinner service for the Empress Catherine of Russia, increased his fame and helped his sales.

'My reason for wanting a large room was to enable me to show various table and dessert services, completely set out on two ranges of tables, six or eight at least; such services are absolutely necessary to be shown in the neatest, genteelest and best method. These articles may every few days be so altered, reversed and transformed as to render the whole a new scene.'

SOURCE 40
Letter from Wedgwood, 1767.

Other products from the Potteries

One of the other new products on which the success of the Potteries was based was the making of tiles (see Source 41). By the late 19th century there was a better understanding of hygiene. Tiles provided a washable, germ-resistant covering which was also attractively decorated. They were used in bathrooms, toilets, fireplaces, washstands, porches, chapels, pubs and foodshops. It is amazing that out of all the smoke and grime of 'The Potteries' came such beautiful objects.

SOURCE 41
Decorative tiles showing characters from Shakespeare's plays.

attainment target 1

1. The reasons for Wedgwood's success are divided up here into: changes in public taste, Wedgwood's abilities, the factory system, new technology and selling. Explain one reason from each section that you think is important.
2. Give one reason for his success which was entirely beyond his control.
3. Give one reason for his success which made use of other people's ideas.
4. Explain how the factory he set up at Etruria combined his own abilities, new technology, meeting changes in public taste, and new approaches to selling.

How were people's working lives affected?

On pages 14–15 we saw that there was a time-lag between new inventions in cotton spinning and cotton weaving. For a while hand-loom weavers grew rich, weaving all the yarn produced in factories. When steam-powered looms were introduced, the hand-loom weavers suffered because machines could weave the cloth much faster and more cheaply. The only way they could compete was to take cuts in their wages (see Source 42). They were just one of the many skilled trades which disappeared with the coming of factory machines. Some early factory machines, such as the first spinning frames (see Source 13, page 10) needed skilled operators. Later machines needed little or no skill at all.

'Many of the weavers cannot provide for themselves and their families sufficient food of the plainest and cheapest kind. They are clothed in rags, they have scarcely any furniture in their houses. Despite their poverty they have full employment; in fact their labour is excessive, often 16 hours a day.'

SOURCE 42
From a Report to Parliament about hand-loom weavers, 1835.

'Be at the works the first in the morning to encourage those who come regularly to time, distinguishing them from the less orderly parts of the work-people by presents or other marks.'

SOURCE 43
Josiah Wedgwood's instructions to his foremen.

Factory discipline

It must have been very hard for people used to working on their own at home, at their own speed, to fit into factory work. The powered machines went on and on, hour after hour, and workers had to keep up with them. Owners of the first factories had strict rules to enforce discipline (see Sources 43 and 44). Workers had to do as they were told or lose their jobs.

Wages, hours and conditions

Wages were usually better than in farmwork but only when the factory was working. If business became slack, workers were laid off, with no income at all. To the new factory-owners the workers were 'hands', labourers to be hired and fired when needed. Hours were long (see Source 45) and the only day off was Sunday.

1 The door of the lodge will be closed ten minutes after the engine starts every morning, and no weaver will be admitted until breakfast time. Any weaver absent during that time shall forfeit 3d [1p] a loom.

2 Weavers leaving the room without the consent of the overlooker shall forfeit 3d.

9 All shuttles, brushes, oilcans, windows etc. if broken shall be paid for.

11 If any hand is seen talking to another, whistling or singing he will be fined 6d [2½p].

SOURCE 44
Factory Rules, extracts, 1844.

At what time in the morning when they were busy did the girls go to the mills?
They have gone about three o'clock in the morning and ended at ten or nearly half-past at night.
Had you not great difficulty in awakening your children at this hour?
Yes, we had to take them up asleep and shake them and dress them.
Have your children ever been strapped?
Yes, every one. The eldest daughter's back was beaten nearly to a jelly.

SOURCE 45
From an enquiry into children's working hours, 1831.

SOURCE 46
Working Cort's puddling furnace: the men had to stir 28 lb (12.7 kg) of metal, then lift it out in four huge balls of hot iron.

Working conditions were often unpleasant. See Source 46 for one of the jobs in the iron industry. Cotton factories were usually kept hot and humid to prevent the threads from breaking.

Children

As we saw on page 8, children had always worked with their families. Some early factories took on large numbers of poor and orphaned children who were made to live in the factory. Many were badly treated and this system was stopped in 1802. In early factories mothers, fathers and children often worked together (Source 47). However, later factories only needed unskilled workers to look after the machines and tie up the threads. Factory-owners could get children to do these jobs for the lowest wages. Parents, often unemployed themselves, were glad of the money. Source 48 shows that these child-workers had no protection from bad conditions.

Dangers

It is clear from many of the pictures in this unit that early factory machines were often dangerous. There were no safety laws and no protective guards on dangerous machines. Some dangers, such as those described in Source 48, were obvious. Others, such as the dangers to health from lead in the paint used to decorate pottery, were not understood.

SOURCE 47
Cotton-spinning mules in a factory.

'A boy aged 16 working at Hemingsley's nail factory at Wolverhampton. Accidents happen there every week, very near; finger ends are continually pinched, sometimes pinched off, or cut off.'

SOURCE 48
Accidents in nail factories, from a Report to Parliament on children's work, 1843.

attainment target 1

1. What changes were there in the places where people worked?
2. What other changes were there in people's working lives?
3. Which aspect of the changes do you think workers would dislike most? Explain your answer.
4. Do you think working in factories was more or less dangerous than working in the domestic system?
5. Who do you think was affected most by the growth of the factory system: skilled workers, women or children? Who do you think was least affected?

How did women's jobs change?

The change from the domestic system to the factory system affected women at least as much as men. For both, factory work meant the loss of freedom, long hours and the unending, clanking, steam-driven machines. For women, working at home fitted well with their traditional task of bringing up the children. It was much harder to combine this task with factory work. Source 49 explains how a woman feels as the factory whistle calls her away from her baby early in the morning.

The change from the domestic system to the factory system could put women in a stronger position than before. Single women had their own wages which gave them some independence. Married women could find themselves the breadwinner for the family if the man could not get work. Men like Lord Shaftesbury (see Source 50) did not like the idea, but women seem to have enjoyed themselves at times.

In early factories families often worked together. By the 1840s the situation was as shown in Source 51: the work of minding the machines is being done by women, children do odd jobs and men supervise them all. If men and women did the same job, women were paid less. For this reason, factory-owners preferred to employ women for most ordinary jobs. The MILLWRIGHTS and mechanics who repaired the machines were more skilled and better paid, and all of them were men.

Oh, the whistle is a-blowing, sleep my bonny bairn,
Oh, the whistle is a-blowing, it's time for me to go,
Oh, the wheels they go a-turning and the noise it makes you scream,
There's a-racing and a-going and the hissing of the steam.

[bairn = baby; some factories had whistles to mark the start of work]

SOURCE 49
Verse from a 19th century song.

'Fifty or sixty females, married and single, form themselves into clubs. They meet together to drink, sing and smoke; they use the lowest, most disgusting language imaginable. Why is it that this is taking place? Because now women have to support their husbands and families, which has the effect of introducing disorder and conflict.'

SOURCE 50
Lord Shaftesbury, speaking in Parliament, 1844.

SOURCE 51
Men, women and children working in a cotton-mill in the 1840s.

SOURCE 52
Servants at a house in Essex in the 1890s.

Other work for women

Many parts of Britain had no factories, yet one in three of all workers was female. Women took whatever work was available locally, nearly always in less well-paid jobs. Some worked down coalmines (see page 26); many worked in agriculture, in gangs or doing seasonal work like hop-picking.

Domestic service

In the 19th century there was a huge increase in the number of women working as domestic servants: cooks, housemaids, nursemaids etc. By 1881 there were over one million of them. People in quite ordinary jobs could afford to employ a servant. A 13 year old maid-of-all-work could be hired for only 1 shilling (5p) a week. At the other end of the scale, the Duke of Westminster had over 300 servants. The household of a landowner can be seen in Source 52. The manservants mainly did outdoor jobs such as looking after the horses. The items held by the men and women show the different jobs they did.

At the top of the scale was the cook or housekeeper, who might be paid £40 a year. Housemaids or kitchenmaids might only get £15 a year. This was less than they would earn in a factory, though their food and some clothing were provided.

Hours of work were long. In many houses jobs like cleaning and laying fires had to be done before the owner got up. This meant an early start. The only time off was one evening a week, one afternoon a month and one week a year. Source 53 describes some of a housemaid's jobs.

A kind and generous master or mistress made all the difference. In large houses, the servants ate in the servant's hall. At Christmas the whole household, servants and all, would join in the celebrations. For country girls from poor families a place in a big house was worth having. On their one week's holiday they would come home with money and perhaps cast-off clothing for their family. Some were sent away from home at the age of 13. Many girls resented the way their employer restricted their lives. They were lonely, had little time off and boyfriends (called 'followers') were forbidden. For all its unpleasantness, factory work seemed preferable to those girls who had a choice.

'Lighted the kitchen fire and swept the floors. Clean'd the steps and shook the mats. Wash'd me and got breakfast. Dusted the rooms and the hall. Rubb'd the brasswork in the WC and cleaned the little window. Clean'd the two copper coal scuttles. Carried the one full o' coals into the dining room. Got the dinner by half past one.

SOURCE 53
From the diary of Hannah Cullwick, a housemaid, 28 September 1871.

Discuss these questions in pairs.

1 Women tried hard to combine a job with caring for their children. What evidence is there on these pages of the problems this can cause?

2 How did the factory system make life harder for women?

3 Discuss where you would have preferred to work: in a factory like Source 51 or as a servant like those in Source 52?

How was more coal produced?

From what you have read in this unit so far, you would expect to see coal production increase in this period. There was the demand for coal from all those steam-engines and furnaces in all those factories. Source 54 shows that coal production did indeed increase. But in the other industries we have looked at, new machines were the main cause of change. They greatly increased the amount produced per worker (their 'productivity'). What about the productivity of miners? Use a calculator and Source 54 to work out the productivity of miners: for each year, divide the amount of coal mined by the number of miners. You will find that it actually fell during these years. What does this tell us about new machines in coalmining?

The miner's job

Source 55 shows an 18th century coalmine; small, RURAL, no more than 50 metres deep. The demand for more coal for industry was met by employing more miners, digging more pits and deeper pits. By 1800, pits 300 metres deep were being sunk. In 1834 Monkwearmouth Colliery, Sunderland, had a SHAFT 500 metres deep.

The job of mining remained much the same: hard, physical labour in terrible conditions (see Sources 56 and 57). Pits were hot, smelly (there were no toilets) and dangerous. The miner cut the coal in seams which were in some places only a few centimetres thick. It was then carried away to the bottom of the shaft to be hauled to the surface. In early years, this was done by women and children, often the miner's family. Later, pit-ponies did the work, spending all their lives underground.

1761	5 million tons	About 16,000 miners
1801	13 million tons	About 40,000 miners
1861	89 million tons	About 300,000 miners
1901	229 million tons	About 950,000 miners

SOURCE 54
Amount of coal produced and numbers of miners in Britain, 1761–1901.

SOURCE 55
Horse-driven 'whim-gin' for hauling coal and miners up and down a pit in Wales.

SOURCE 56
Miner at work in Wales, about 1900.

> At intervals along the passage I found it closed by wooden doors, each attended by a boy, who opened it for the passing of the wagons and then shut it again. These form part of the arrangements for ventilating the mine. At length we came to two human figures, almost naked; the one wielding a pick against the solid wall of coal, the other shovelling the resulting loose coal into a wagon. Having taken a hasty peep at the vast furnace used for the ventilation of the pit, I stepped once more into the metal tub and was hoisted to the upper world.

SOURCE 57
Description of a visit down a Durham coal mine in 1844.

SOURCE 58
Steam-engine at a pit in about 1790.

New problems and dangers

Bigger and deeper pits brought new problems and dangers for the miners. Water entered the mines, causing flooding. Steam-engines were used to pump the water out, making deep mining possible (see Source 58).

Dangerous gases built up in mines and could cause huge explosions. One solution was to have a large fire burning below one shaft, sucking a draught of fresh air through the mine. Trapdoors ensured that the air circulated properly. Small children, as young as three or four, had the job of opening and shutting these doors (see Source 57).

Explosions were often caused by the candles miners used to see by. In 1815 Sir Humphry Davy and George Stephenson invented a 'safety lamp'. This gave a light without the heat which caused explosions. Some say it saved miners' lives. Others say it encouraged mine-owners to make miners work in unsafe conditions. Certainly, terrible accidents continued to happen. On 12 December 1866, 340 men and boys went down the Oaks pit, Barnsley. An explosion killed all but six of them and all 40 of the pit-ponies in the mine. Source 59 shows a second explosion at the colliery.

Another hazard was the dust which miners breathed in. After a few years, their lungs became clogged with it and they became unable to breathe properly.

SOURCE 59
Oaks Colliery disaster, Barnsley, Yorkshire, 1866.

1. What new inventions were used in the coal industry in these years?
2. How did they affect the job of the miner?
3. Why didn't they have much effect on the productivity of miners?
4. What effect do you think a dangerous job like mining would have on the people who did it?

Making links

We have already seen several links between industries in this unit. Skilled ironworking enabled James Watt to make his improved steam-engine; steam-power enabled the cotton industry to expand, and so on.

Engineering

The link industry was engineering. Engineers were the people who made and repaired the machines used by other industries. Bateman and Sharrard's (see Source 60) made steam-engines for the cotton mills of Manchester and Lancashire. In turn, they used the better quality iron coming from the new, improved ironworks. They used steam-engines themselves to drive their lathes, hammers and the BELLOWS for their foundry. And, of course, they used coal.

In Source 61 you can see (rather exaggerated in size) some of the range of industrial items made at Peel and Williams' foundry. Similar engineering firms in Leeds made machines for the woollen industry, and in Birmingham for the metal trades of the Midlands.

The diagram (Source 62) shows other links between the iron, coal and steam industries.

'Mr Sharrard is a very able engineer, who has improved upon and brought the steam-engine to great perfection. Most of those that are used in and about Manchester are of their make and fitting up.'

SOURCE 60
Written in 1795 by John Aiken.

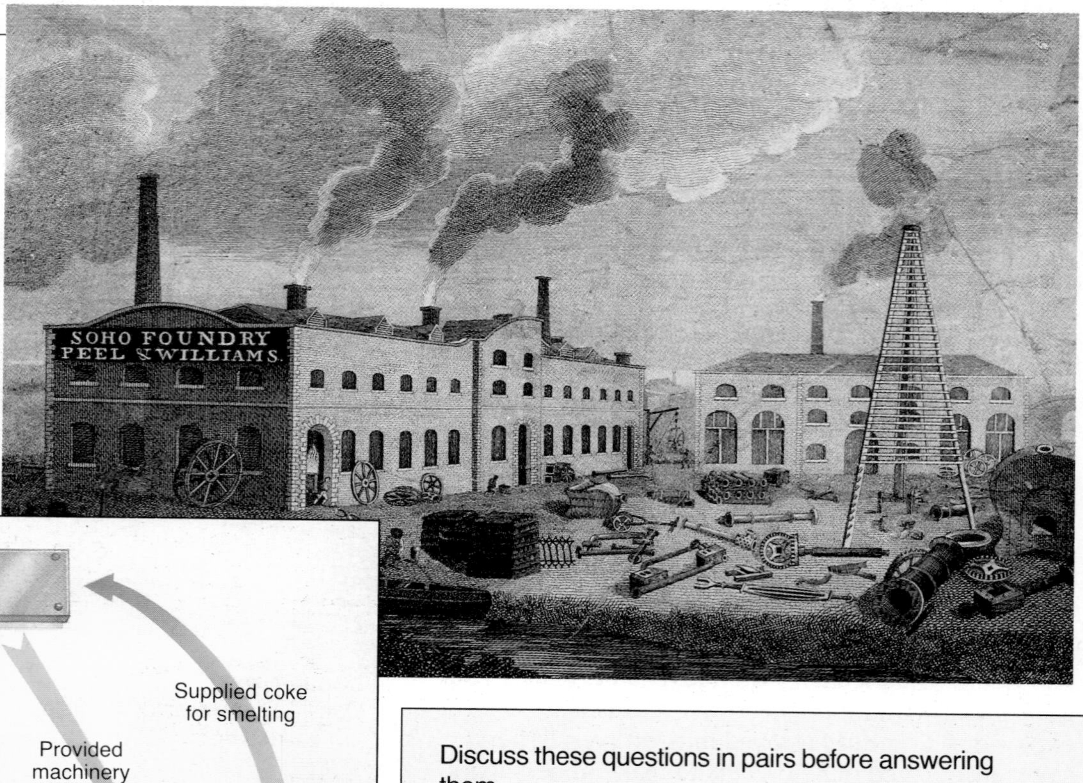

SOURCE 61
Peel and Williams Works in Manchester in 1814.

SOHO FOUNDRY
PEEL & WILLIAMS.

SOURCE 62
Diagram showing links between the iron, coal and steam industries.

IRON
Supplied air-blast and powered hammers
Provided better castings
Provided machinery
Supplied coke for smelting
STEAM
Powered pumping and winding engines
COAL
Supplied fuel

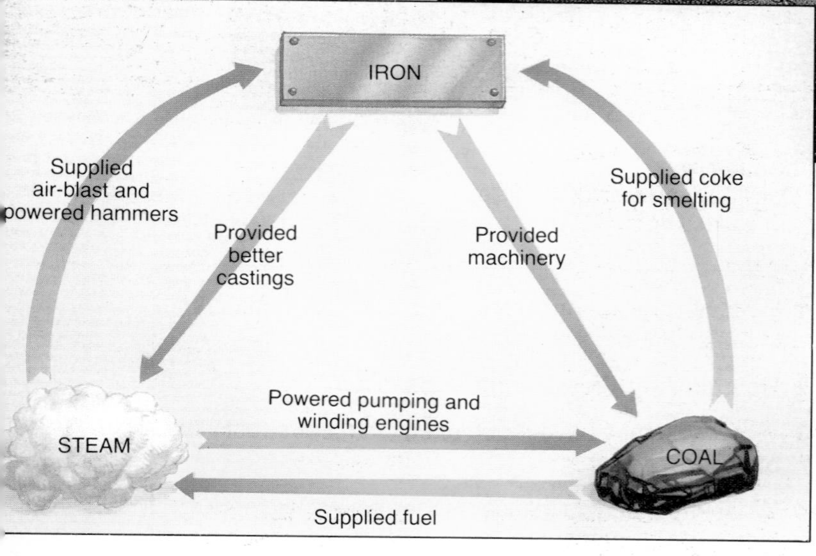

Discuss these questions in pairs before answering them.

1 What other links between iron, coal and steam can you think of?

2 Can you add the cotton industry to the diagram (Source 62), making links between it and the iron, coal and steam industries?

3 Can you add the engineering industry to this diagram in the same way?

Summing up

Despite all the machines described in this unit, the most important thing to sum up is: how were people affected?

1 Compare Source 63 with Source 10, page 9. What does it tell you about changes to the working lives of the people of Britain?

2 Do you think these changes amount to an 'industrial revolution'?

3 From what you have read in this book so far, do you think these changes were for the better or for the worse?

4 Compare Sources 64 and 65. Look for the differences between them. What differences are here in the things you can see: the amount of iron being hammered, the size of the machines, the surroundings?

5 What differences are there in the people? The number of people, their age and sex, how they seem to feel about what they are doing?

6 In what ways do Sources 64 and 65 sum up this unit?

Manufacturing	3,200,000
Mining	300,000
Building	500,000
Trade and transport	1,500,000
Domestic service	1,300,000
Agriculture	2,100,000

SOURCE 63
Numbers of people in various jobs in Britain, 1851.

SOURCE 64
Painting of a water-powered tilt-hammer, 1772, by Joseph Wright of Derby.

SOURCE 65
James Nasmyth's own painting of his steam-hammer, invented in 1840.

UNIT 2

The British Empire

AIMS

Many books on this period only deal with what went on in Britain. But, as we shall see in this unit, British industrialisation depended on buying and selling goods across the world.

By 1750 Britain was already trading on a large scale, including trading in slaves. Wealth from trade helped to start the industrial changes described in unit 1. This unit looks at how Britain came to rule large parts of the world, known as the British Empire. We shall also see how these worldwide links affected life in Britain.

Think of the food you have eaten in the past few days: which items were grown in Britain and which were grown abroad? What else is there in your home or classroom which was made abroad?

We expect to see goods from all over the world in our shops nowadays. In 1750 this worldwide market was only just beginning. The voyages of 16th and 17th century European seamen brought most of the world into contact with Europe. All sorts of new products became available. There was tea from China, tobacco from North America, sugar from the West Indies, silk and spices from the East Indies and cotton from India. At first these were luxury items, but they soon became part of everyone's life. For example, tea began to replace beer as the everyday drink of most English people, and smoking became a popular habit.

A TRADING NATION

The map (Source 1) shows that this world trade was dominated by Europe and that Britain had a large share of it. Her Atlantic trade was slightly more than France's; both were now ahead of Spain which had once controlled trade to the Americas. The Dutch had a big trade with the East, but so did Britain and France.

SOURCE 1
Map showing value of world trade to Europe in the 1770s.

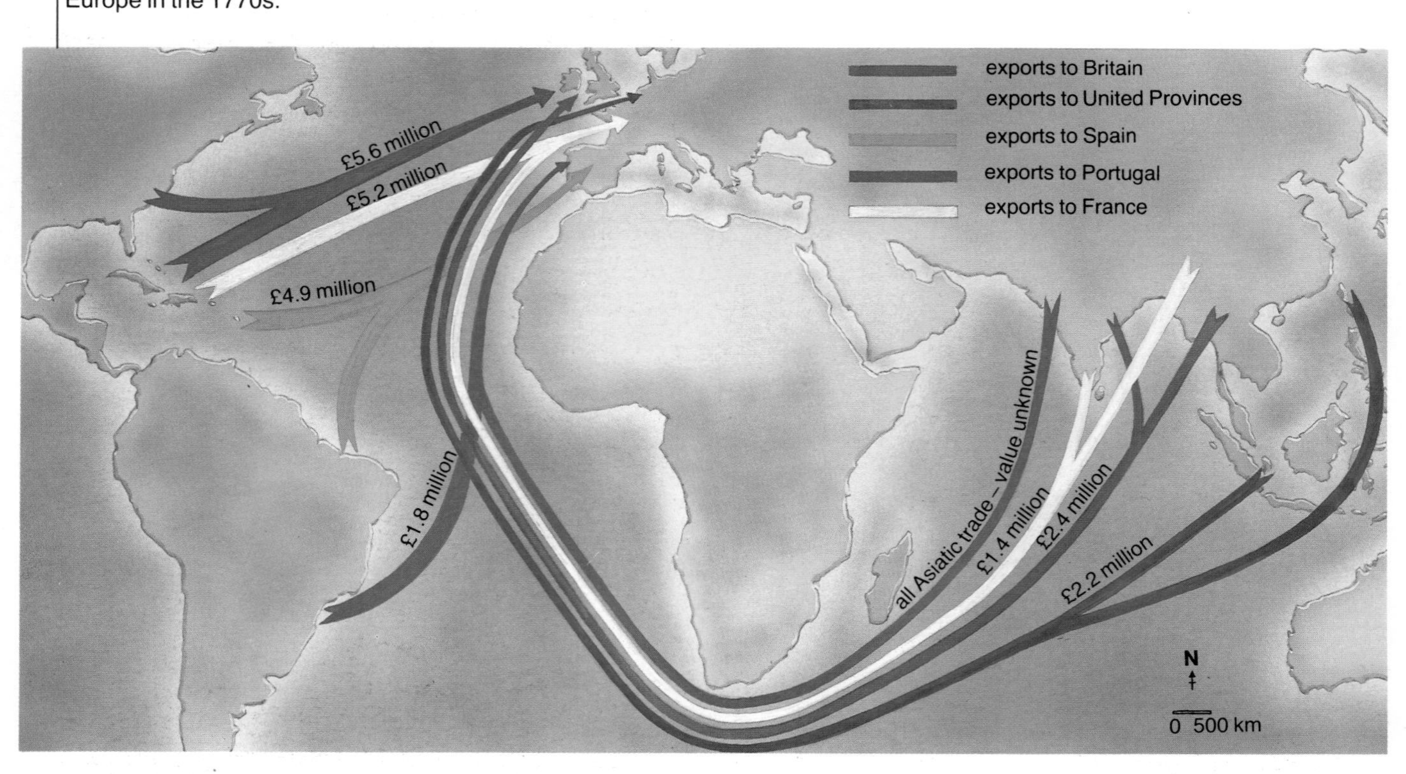

British colonies

The only large amounts of land held by Britain in 1750 were in North America, the 13 COLONIES. Apart from them, there were some Caribbean islands and some TRADING POSTS in India and Africa. At that time Britain had no intention of conquering and ruling other lands.

The government knew the importance of trade, however, and was prepared to go to war to increase it. In 1763, by the end of the Seven Years' War, Britain had made tremendous gains in various parts of the world. The French were removed from most of North America, including Canada. Britain gained several sugar-growing islands in the Caribbean and increased her influence in India. The patriotic song 'Rule Britannia' (Source 2), composed at the time, shows British feelings.

'The natural products of Britain do not at most amount to a quarter of her riches. The rest she owes to her colonies and her people, who by the transport and exchange of the riches of other countries, continually add to their own.'

SOURCE 3
The French writer Le Blanc, describing the importance of trade to Britain, writing in 1747.

Trading wealth

To foreign observers, like the author of Source 3, trade was the main source of the wealth of the country. Many people were involved. There were probably 6,000 merchants and 100,000 seamen. Ports on the west coast of Britain, such as Liverpool, Glasgow and Bristol (see Source 4), grew. Wealthy merchants had money to invest in new industrial enterprises. They put up money for canals, mines and factories. Abraham Darby, for example, borrowed money from friends in Bristol to help start his ironworks at Coalbrookdale (see page 17).

When Britain first, at Heaven's command,
Arose from out the azure main
This was the charter, the charter of the land,
And guardian angels sang the strain:
Rule Britannia, Britannia rules the waves
Britons never, never, never shall be slaves.

[azure main = blue sea]

SOURCE 2
From the song 'Rule Britannia'.

Look at Source 4 with a partner. How much can you tell about the trade of Bristol from this source? Keep questioning the picture until you have 'squeezed it dry' for evidence. For example:
How are goods being taken from ships to warehouses?
What kinds of goods can you see?
What signs of prosperity are there?

SOURCE 4
Bristol Quay in 1720.

Why did the slave trade develop?

The first colonies in America did not have slaves. Colonists used native American workers or white workers shipped out from Europe, often as an alternative to prison. However, growing and processing crops such as cotton, tobacco and sugar needed large numbers of workers. Native Americans were dying of European diseases by the thousand. The colonists' answer to the shortage of workers was to import black slaves from West Africa. Over 10 million black slaves were taken from Africa to work on PLANTATIONS in America before the trade was abolished in the 19th century.

> As the slaves come down to Fida from the inland country they are put into a prison near the beach. When the Europeans are to receive them they are brought out on to a large plain, where the ship's surgeons examine every part of them. Such as are declared good and sound are marked on the breast with a red-hot iron, imprinting the mark of the French, English or Dutch companies. The branded slaves are then returned to their former prison where they await shipment, sometimes 10–15 days.

SOURCE 6
Description of slaves on the coast of Africa, written in the 18th century.

> 'She had taken in 336 males and 226 females. The space between decks was so low that they sat between each other's legs, so close that there was no possibility of their lying down or changing their positions day or night. This was when the thermometer was standing at 89 degrees [89° Fahrenheit = 32° Celsius].'

SOURCE 7
Captain Newton's description of conditions on board his slaveship.

SOURCE 8
Irons used on slaves.

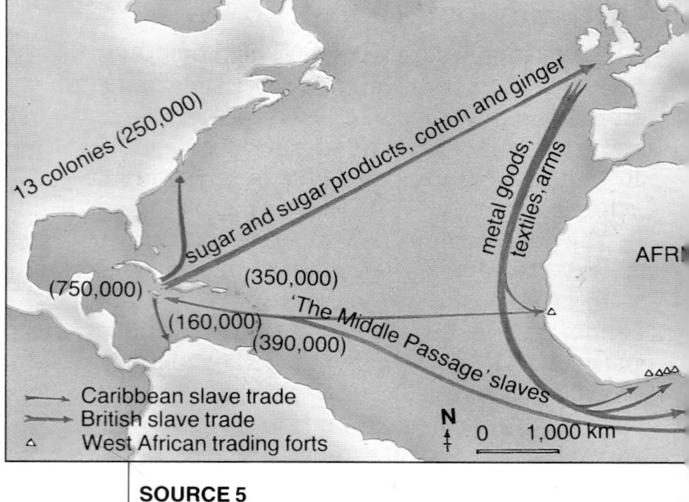

SOURCE 5
Map of the 'triangular trade', showing numbers of slaves TRANSPORTED.

The map (Source 5) shows the three stages of the 'triangular trade', as it was called. Manufactured goods, such as cloth and guns, were used to buy slaves from their African masters. What happened at a slave-dealing fort on the West African coast is described in Source 6. Slaves were then loaded on to ships and taken across to the Caribbean islands or to North or South America. This was the dreaded 'middle passage', on which up to a million slaves may have died. To the slaveship-owners, slaves were just goods to be sold. The more they could cram into the holds of their ships the bigger their profit. Conditions on a slaveship on the 'middle passage' are described in Source 7. Irons such as those in Source 8 had to be used to stop slaves attacking the crew.

On arrival, the slaves would be sold by auction (see Source 9). Meanwhile the merchant ships would be loaded with valuable cargo for the trip back to Europe.

Slaves resisted this treatment in a number of ways. Many committed suicide. Runaway slaves in Jamaica, called **maroons**, set up little communities in the hills. There were slave rebellions and communities of runaway slaves in several colonies. Some slaves managed to buy their freedom or were given freedom by their owner.

Britain and the slave trade

Britain was well placed to take part in this trade. There were plenty of merchant ships; industry was producing the goods to sell in West Africa; there was an increasing demand for colonial products such as sugar. In 1713, Britain gained the right (called an **asiento**) to supply 4,800 slaves a year to the Spanish colonies in America. As demand for colonial products grew, so did the slave trade. By the later 18th century 60,000 slaves a year were being carried, half of them in British ships. Profits from slavery and the slave trade flowed into British ports and were invested in British industry.

An increasing number of black people came to live in Britain. There were black communities in London and other British ports by the 18th century. A black sailor in the Royal Navy can be seen in Source 10.

James Madison, who later became President of the USA, said that a slave could make him $257 profit a year, at a cost of only $12. From the 18th century on, many people worked to abolish the slave trade. British slave-owners also made big profits out of slavery and opposed its abolition. Slavery was not abolished in British territory until 1833.

ACTIVITY

Divide into groups of three. Each group is an anti-slavery society. Prepare a leaflet to persuade people that slavery is wrong and should be abolished. Your teacher is a firm believer in the slave trade and makes quite a lot of money out of slave-worked plantations. Try to persuade her/him to change her/his mind.

SOURCE 9
A slave auction in Virginia, USA.

SOURCE 10
Picture of the death of Admiral Nelson, 1805, showing a black sailor on 'HMS Victory'.

Why did Britain gain an empire?

The British Empire of the 18th century was mainly a trading empire. Trading companies, not the British government, ran many of the colonies. The Hudson's Bay Company, set up in 1670, ran much of northern Canada. The Royal Africa Company, 1672, dealt with West Africa. Most important of all, the East India Company, set up back in 1600, ruled an increasing part of India. In fact, British politicians at this time did not want an empire. They thought that governing far-off lands was expensive and unnecessary.

In several parts of the world British merchants went on trading profitably without taking on the responsibilities of government. The American colonies became independent in 1783 but the USA continued to trade heavily with Britain. In 1793 the British tried to persuade the Emperor of China to trade. He refused (see Source 11), but in 1842 China was forced to open up to western trade. All the Europeans had to do was to govern 'treaty ports' as they were called. From these ports, like Hong Kong, Britain could trade with all of China. Britain also traded widely in South America without having any colonies there.

So how did Britain acquire the territories shown in Source 12? Some were taken to stop anyone else getting them. In three voyages between 1768 and 1780, Captain Cook mapped much of Australia and New Zealand. In 1788 a colony was established in Australia, mainly for convicts. In 1819 Sir Stamford Raffles set up the colony of Singapore, to counter Dutch influence in the East Indies.

Some territories were taken as part of the war against Napoleon and his allies, waged from 1793 to 1815. Trinidad and what is now Guyana were seized from Spain. The Dutch colony in South Africa was taken in 1795. British bases were set up on Malta in 1799, and on Corfu.

> 'We need nothing from you. We have all things. The manufactures of your country are not the slightest use to us. It is your duty to obey our wishes. Everlasting obedience to the Dragon throne of China will bring peace and riches to your land.'

SOURCE 11
Reply of the Chinese Emperor to Lord Macartney who had gone to persuade the Chinese to trade with Britain, 1793.

SOURCE 12
Map showing the growth of the British Empire, 1763–1870.

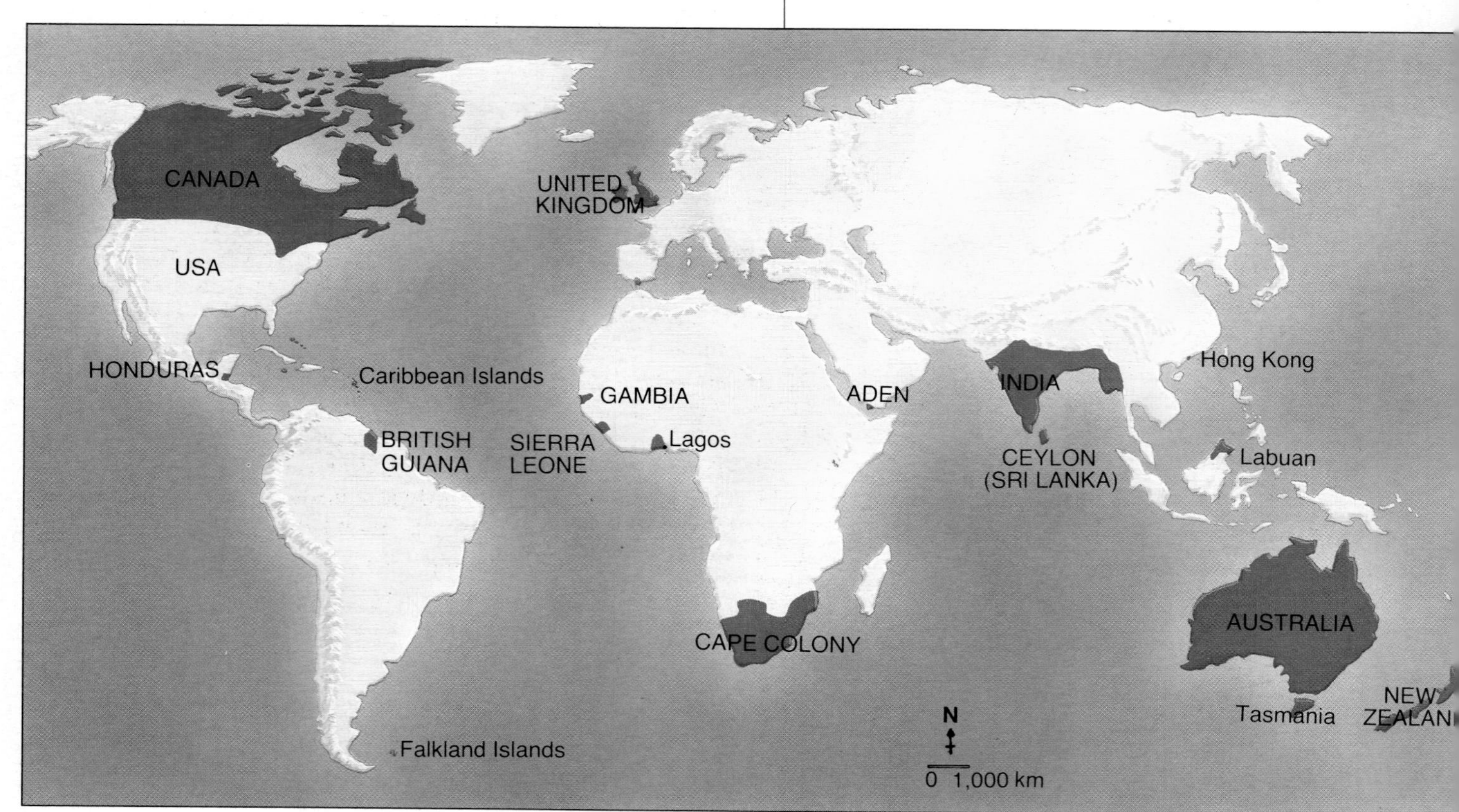

British attitudes towards the idea of an empire began to change. In 1850 Lord Russell spoke of the 'high and holy work' of extending British influence across the world. This idea that the British were a superior race, with a mission to bring other races up to British standards, was gaining strength. To David Livingstone British science, medicine and religion were benefits he had to bring to what he called 'the dark continent', Africa. He made a series of journeys across Central Africa (see Source 13) and died there in 1863.

Another reason for the growth of the empire was emigration (see also page 76). Between 1815 and 1912 10 million people emigrated to British territories overseas.

SOURCE 13
David Livingstone's PADDLE-STEAMER on the River Shire, 1858.

Ruling the Empire

So the British colonies grew and grew. New lands and more people meant that the government in London had to take more control. Trading companies were for trade, not for governing millions of people.

Canada grew rapidly. In 1812 Lord Selkirk was granted 250,000 square kilometres of land in Manitoba for Scottish SETTLERS. In 1865 the Canadian Pacific Railway linked east and west by rail and in 1867 Canada became a DOMINION with its own government.

SOURCE 14
British merchant, John Mowbray, in 1790, with his Indian servant and business agent.

Australia's population grew. The flow of convicted criminals from the crowded British cities increased to over 3,000 a year in the 1820s. Many were transported for life for very minor offences. A new settlement, Melbourne, was named after the Prime Minister in 1837. It soon had 10,000 people and 80 times that many sheep. New Zealand had a quarter of a million people by 1860.

In South Africa the old Dutch settlers hated their new British masters. In 1837 they made the 'Great Trek' northwards to found new colonies further inland.

India saw a sharp decline in the influence of the old trading company, the East India Company. The government in Britain was convinced that Company 'NABOBS', like John Mowbray (Source 14), were too powerful and corrupt. The passing of the India Act 1784 set up a Board of Control to supervise the work of the Company. Then it had its monopoly of trade with India and China taken away. As the British took over more and more of India the cost of government increased. In the 1830s and 1840s, Governors General tried to introduce British-style law and education. The Indian people resisted this interference in their way of life. In 1857 thousands of Indian soldiers MUTINIED, attacked the British and took over several areas (the First War of Independence). The next year, the British government took over India completely from the East India Company.

Sailing ships

How did the Industrial Revolution affect shipping? All the trade we have looked at in this unit had to be carried by sea. What were ships like at this time?

The battle of Trafalgar, 1805, was fought by wooden sailing ships. Apart from being a bit bigger, they were not much different from sailing ships of 100 years earlier. Surely the inventions of the Industrial Revolution could improve ships? Steam power had obvious advantages over sail. (Can you think of some?) The first steam-engine was used on a ship in the 1780s and in 1812 Henry Bell's *Comet* ran a successful steam service on the Clyde in Scotland. By 1821 there were 188 steamers in use. They were used mainly as tugs and estuary ferries. These paddle-steamers could travel regardless of the wind or tide. By the 1840s there were some 1,400 coastal steamboat services, visiting 90 ports around Britain.

But there were severe disadvantages in using these early steamships for ocean journeys. Firstly, they were unreliable, so could not be trusted for long trips. Secondly, paddle-steamers have difficulty in rough seas as the paddles are lifted out of the water. Thirdly, they used so much coal on long journeys that there was no room for cargo or passengers. The *Savannah* made the journey from New York to Liverpool in 1819 using both sail and steam but the experiment was not repeated. Sail continued to dominate international trade.

SOURCE 15
A clipper under full sail.

SOURCE 16
Brunel's steamship, the *Great Britain*, being launched in 1843.

Clippers

The fastest commercial sailing ships ever built were the clippers (see Source 15). They could sail at 16 knots (nautical miles per hour) and do the journey from Australia to Britain in 60 days. They were mainly used to bring the valuable tea cargoes fresh from China. Their success depended on a mixture of old and new technology. They had iron frames, with wooden planks, so were large enough to carry a good cargo. They used steam-winches to control a huge amount of sail, which gave them their speed.

Brunel

Having designed the Great Western Railway from London to Bristol, Isambard Kingdom Brunel was keen to offer a service on to New York. In 1838 his *Great Western* was launched, a paddle-steamer which made the journey across the Atlantic in 14 days.

His *Great Britain* (Source 16), launched in 1845, had an iron hull. There was plenty of room for cargo. It also had a screw propeller, stronger and safer than paddles. His final answer to the problem was the *Great Eastern*, built in 1858. At 20,000 tons it was the largest ship ever built. It had sails, paddles and a screw propeller. It was so large that although it burnt 300 tons of coal a day, it still had room for 4,000 passengers and 5,000 tons of cargo. However, the design was way ahead of its time; its owners went BANKRUPT, and no one copied it.

Steam takes over

Brunel's pioneering designs, and new inventions and materials, led to the triumph of steam in the second half of the 19th century. John Elder's compound engine, invented in 1854, was more efficient. This meant ships needed much less coal. The Suez Canal, opened in 1869, was not used by sailing ships as towing was too expensive. Steamships benefited from the much shorter journey from Britain, through the Canal, to India and Australia.

By the 1860s much cheaper steel was being made (see page 19). Steel ships could be built lighter, stronger and larger than before. Although wooden sailing ships were still widely used, the future lay with steel and steam. By 1870 more than half the world's tonnage of ships was British.

SOURCE 17
A paddle-steamer at the opening of the Suez Canal, 1869.

Ocean voyages

Larger ships meant that new standards of luxury could be provided for passengers. Smaller, older ships and sailing ships offered cheap fares to poorer people at quite a different standard. Sources 17, 18, 19 and 20 tell you something about ocean travel at this time.

SOURCE 19
The saloon of Brunel's ship the *Great Eastern*.

'We are given our water every morning. This morning it was taken from a fresh cask and it stank so that we could not drink it and were obliged to boil it and put peppermint with it. We can bake bread every three days if we like, for a penny a loaf.'

SOURCE 20
Conditions for steerage passengers crossing the Atlantic, 1848.

At dinner the ship was struck by a heavy sea which created quite a commotion among the dishes, for they were all mixed up together. You have to hold on to your plate to keep it near you, hold on to your glass of water to avoid the unnecessary luxury of a shower-bath.

During the night another gale sprung up. While on the main deck got several drenchings for the sea is coming right over the rail.

SOURCE 18
An account of a storm at sea in the 1850s.

attainment target 3

1. What do you think it would be like to travel on the *Great Eastern* (Source 19)?
2. How does Source 18 add to our understanding of ocean travel in the 19th century?
3. Which of Sources 17, 18 or 19 is the most useful for finding out about the size of ocean-going steamships in the 19th century? Explain your answer.
4. In what ways do the people in Source 20 seem to have different facilities?
5. How useful is Source 20 for finding out about 'steerage' passengers? What else would you like to know about their trip?
6. Both Sources 17 and 19 were produced to show their subjects at their best. How does this affect your opinion of ocean travel in the 19th century?

How important was trade and the Empire to British industry?

Building the big steel ships described on page 37 was a whole new industry. The *Great Eastern* (Source 21) was exceptional for its time, but by 1900 many ships of that size were being built. One third of Britain's steel output at that time went to build ships. Shipbuilding yards were established on the Clyde, the Tyne, at Belfast and Barrow-in-Furness, with a huge workforce for each ship.

Look at Source 4 on page 31. The tremendous increase in Britain's trade since 1720 needed much larger docks and harbours. Source 22 shows one of London's great 19th century docks: the West India Docks. The dock on the left is a timber dock; the other two are surrounded by warehouses, for exports (left), and imports (right). Other huge docks were built at Liverpool, Swansea, Cardiff, Bristol and Glasgow.

SOURCE 21
Building the *Great Eastern* at Millwall Docks, London, 1857.

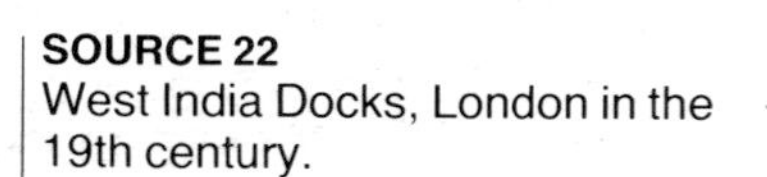

SOURCE 22
West India Docks, London in the 19th century.

Imports

Source 23 shows how much imports grew over the period. Some, like tea or furs, were sold to the public as they were. Others, like tobacco, sugar, cotton, tropical timber or cocoa, went to factories in Britain. Here they were made into the things people would buy. They were then sold in Britain or exported abroad. For example, cocoa was becoming a popular drink in the 19th century, especially among those who opposed the sale of alcohol. Cadbury's and Fry's

	Exports	Imports
1720s	£7.5 million	£7.0 million
1760s	£15.0 million	£10.5 million
1800s	£37.5 million	£28.5 million
1840s	£141.5 million	£79.5 million

SOURCE 23
Values of British imports and exports.

factories turned the raw cocoa into drinking or eating chocolate. These imports were therefore raw materials. Business people wanted the Empire to grow in order to supply Britain with cheap raw materials. Some of them set up their own plantations to produce these raw materials. Source 24 shows one of the tea plantations in Ceylon (now Sri Lanka) belonging to Lipton's, a Scottish tea importer.

The Empire could also provide cheap food. The larger ships, and refrigerated ships, being built by the late 19th century made these imports possible: meat from South America, grain from North America, butter and cheese from Australia and New Zealand. Bananas and pineapples were a common sight in British shops by 1900.

SOURCE 24
Lipton's tea plantations, Ceylon (now Sri Lanka).

Exports

British settlers in the colonies were a ready market for British goods (see Source 25). But booming British industry needed big markets. By 1850, Britain was producing two thirds of the world's coal, half the iron, five sevenths of the steel, half the cotton goods and two fifths of the hardware. Britain could not use all this at home; only a growing Empire could keep up with growing British industry. Exports of all kinds of products, from clothes to railways, were essential. Source 26 shows a British-made railway in Ceylon.

In unit 1 it was the cotton industry that gave us the most remarkable example of industrial change. It is worth looking at cotton again to see how it fitted into British trade. All the raw material for the cotton industry was imported, mostly from the USA. Once turned into cloth, two thirds of it was exported.

'Woollens, linen, silk, iron, brass, leather, glass, china, clocks, watches, jewels, gold and silver, lace, medicine, gunpowder, bricks, paint, candles, swords, books, toys, stationery, cutlery, haberdashery, household goods, furniture, clothes . . . in short all things necessary for life and almost the whole is British manufacture.'

SOURCE 25
Goods bought by Europeans in the West Indies, 1763.

India had a thriving cotton industry when the British arrived. Her cotton goods were imported into Britain until this was stopped in 1700 to protect the British cotton industry. From 1813, cheap Lancashire cotton goods were sold in India. The Indian cotton industry could not compete and collapsed. India became just another huge market for British-made goods.

SOURCE 26
British-built railway in Ceylon, 1893.

attainment target 1

1. Which British industries used imports from the colonies?
2. Explain why the Indian cotton industry collapsed.
3. How did imports from abroad affect the things British people ate and drank in the years 1750 to 1900?
4. Cheap raw materials | Cheap food | Bigger, faster ships | Large export market
   Choose two of these items and show how they assisted the British Industrial Revolution.
5. Which of the four items in question **4** had the biggest effect on the cotton industry?
6. Explain what the British Empire has to do with all four of the items in question **4**.

UNIT 3

Transport for all

AIMS

This unit is about transport: the way people and goods are carried around the country. We shall see that new ideas and inventions brought great changes, on the roads, on water and on railways. Better transport was closely linked to the needs of industry, but we will see that the changes also had major effects on people's lives.

It is not true that people did not move around the country in the past. Travel was very difficult, however, because the roads were so bad. Source 1 shows what the roads were like and Source 2 shows that even the Queen could get stuck in the mud. Very few people travelled by carriage for this reason. Most people who could afford it rode on horseback. Those who could not, walked.

SOURCE 1
View of Nottingham and the Trent, 1695.

'We set out at six in the morning and did not get out of the carriages (except when we were overturned or stuck fast in the mud), till we arrived at our journey's end 14 hours later.'

SOURCE 2
Queen Anne describes a journey from Windsor to Petworth, a distance of 64 kilometres, in 1704.

Carrying goods

Goods were carried about the country in a variety of ways. On the roads, slow lumbering wagons like the one in Source 3 were used. Their wheels had to be wide by law, as they feared narrow wheels dug up the roads.

Where the hills made it impossible to use wheeled vehicles, PACKHORSES were used. The busy cloth industry of Lancashire and Yorkshire used long trains of packhorses to get cloth to market. Each horse carried a 'pack' of wool or cloth on its back.

Animals were often driven to market, sometimes over hundreds of kilometres. Wide, green DROVE ROADS led out of Wales into England and were used by drovers with herds of Welsh black cattle. They travelled about 16 kilometres a day, grazing as they went. Even geese were sometimes driven to market in London from East Anglia.

Rivers were used a great deal for transport. Source 1 shows a barge on the Trent. Source 4 explains how important river transport was in eastern England. Heavy, bulky items could be carried on water more easily. Rivers were often dredged or straightened to make them easier to use. It was the good transport on the River Severn which made Coalbrookdale such an attractive site for Abraham Darby (see page 17).

'Great quantities of corn are carried down by barges to Lynn. By the rivers the merchants of Lynn supply about six counties with their goods, especially wine and coal. All heavy goods are brought by water from London . . . first to the port of Lynn and then in barges up the rivers.'

SOURCE 4
Daniel Defoe's description of King's Lynn, 1724.

About half a century ago the heavy goods passing through Leicester for London and the South, and on the great routes to Leeds and Manchester, did not require more than about one wagon a day each way. One weekly wagon to and fro served Coventry, Warwick and so on to Bristol and the West of England.

SOURCE 5
Trade from Leicester in the 18th century, described in 1828.

SOURCE 3
18th century wagon at a wayside inn.

Why did transport have to improve?

In unit 1 we saw that production of all kinds of goods was increasing fast by the late 18th century. Expanding industry needed cheap, reliable transport of bulky goods such as coal, iron, clay and stone. It needed to be able to sell its products over a wide area, and it needed fast transport for business people.

Source 5 explains just how small the amount of cross-country transport was before the Industrial Revolution. On these pages you can see that there was some transport but it was slow, unreliable and expensive. Roads were often totally impassable, especially in winter. River transport was cheap, but rivers do not always go where you want them to go. The Midlands, particularly, was short of usable rivers. Carrying heavy items such as coal by road could cost 10d (4p) per ton per mile. At this rate its price doubled in 10 miles. No one would buy it so it was not worth expanding production. To grow, industry needed much better transport.

Discuss your answers to these questions in pairs.

1. Which kinds of transport are shown in these pages?
2. What were they used for: people or goods? What kinds of goods?
3. What were the disadvantages of each? Think about: speed, reliability, cost, convenience.

Would better roads solve the problem?

The reason the roads were so bad is that no one bothered to repair them properly. Nowadays local and national governments build and repair roads. At that time everyone had to work for six days a year on the roads. Often all they did was to tip a few stones into the worst of the ruts. One answer was for local business people and landowners to form a 'trust' to build turnpikes. A turnpike is a section of road with gates across it (see Source 6). All road users had to pay a toll to pass through the gates (see Source 7). The money was used to improve the road.

The first turnpike was set up in 1663 but the number increased greatly after 1750. By 1830 about 35,400 kilometres (22,000 miles) of road were operated by turnpike trusts.

SOURCE 6
Tollhouse and turnpike gate.

Roadbuilders

The turnpike trusts could raise money but they did not really know how to build a fast, smooth road. Travellers were still lucky to achieve 11–13 kilometres per hour on a journey and complaints about the roads continued. From the 1770s onwards three road engineers began to make real improvements to the condition of the roads.

John Metcalf was blind. He took great care over the foundations of the roads he built in northern England.

Thomas Telford built canals as well as roads. From 1801 Irish MPs began to sit in the Parliament at Westminster. They were disgusted at the road they had to travel from where the ferry landed, at Holyhead in North Wales, to London. They had the power to make things happen. Telford rebuilt the route with gentler gradients and better bridges, including the elegant one over the Menai Straits in North Wales (Source 8). Altogether Telford built 1,600 kilometres of road with carefully graded layers of stones.

'Turnpikes or tollbars have been set up on the great roads of England, beginning at London, at which all carriages, cattle and travellers are obliged to pay a toll. That is to say, a horse a penny, a coach threepence, a cart fourpence, a wagon sixpence.'

SOURCE 7
From Daniel Defoe's travels, 1724.

James McAdam felt that Telford's methods were too expensive. He built his roads with solid foundations and a covering of small stones. By 1820 he and his sons were responsible for 3,200 kilometres of road.

SOURCE 8
The Menai Suspension Bridge, designed by Thomas Telford, on the London–Holyhead road, opened 1826.

SOURCE 9
The Godalming and Guildford stagecoach. Note the number of outside passengers.

	1760	1830
Norwich	23 hrs	12 hrs
Bath	30 hrs	12 hrs
Manchester	46 hrs	19 hrs
Edinburgh	160 hrs	43 hrs

SOURCE 10
Journey times from London, 1760 and 1830.

Stagecoaches

Better road surfaces meant that coaches could go at faster speeds (Source 9). At every 'stage', as it was called, the four horses pulling the stagecoach were changed, usually at an inn. By using fresh horses, speeds of 16km per hour could be kept up.

The fastest coaches on the road were the mailcoaches. In 1784 John Palmer offered to run a stagecoach to carry the mail between London and Bath. It was a great success. Business and industry needed quick, reliable ways of getting letters around the country. The coaches were black and maroon, carrying only seven passengers, four inside and three on top. The armed guard carried a horn to alert tollgate keepers that they were coming so that the gate could be opened. Drivers carried watches, set and sealed at the beginning of the journey, to keep them to time.

The design of coaches improved, so that they could go faster and carry more people. By the 'golden age' of coach travel, the 1820s and 1830s, there were 700 mailcoach and 3,300 other coach routes in Britain. They were centred on London and the great coaching inns. William Chaplin owned six of these inns, 1,800 horses and 64 coaches, employing 2,000 people. Journey times shrank enormously (see Source 10).

In our day stagecoaches have become a cosy picture from the past, popular on Christmas cards. In fact, travel by stagecoach was often very uncomfortable, particularly for those outside. You had to hang on tight and there was no protection from the weather; sometimes passengers died of exposure. Most of all, it was extremely expensive (see Source 11). At that time an ordinary labourer might earn 50p a week, a skilled worker £1.

Went to the Angel Inn and at 7 o'clock in the evening, myself, Nancy and brother went in the heavy coach for London. For three people's fare I paid £4.50. For extra luggage 75p. We had a pleasant night of travelling. We breakfasted very early but where I know not. I paid 15p. To the coachman that drove us halfway I gave 15p. We all got to London safe and well (thank God) at 3 o'clock this afternoon. To the last coachman I gave 15p.

[Prices changed to modern money]

SOURCE 11
From the diary of Parson Woodforde, 1786.

1. Use the sources on these pages to discuss with a partner what it was like to travel in, or on, a stagecoach. Think of five key words to describe the experience.
2. Did people at the time feel differently about stagecoach travel? In what ways?
3. Do you think toll roads are a good way of raising money for modern road improvements?

Cheap transport: canals

Even on a road with a smooth surface one horse can only pull a weight of about half a ton; it can pull up to 30 tonnes on a boat. People had known this for centuries. Rivers were well used for FREIGHT and even some canals had been built.

The great age of canal building, however, began with the Duke of Bridgewater's canal, completed in 1761. The Duke owned a coalmine at Worsley, only 8 miles from the growing city of Manchester. His problem was that the cost of carrying coal by packhorse into Manchester made it too expensive. The Duke hired James Brindley to make a canal link. Brindley proved a genius at working out ways of building canals. He made it start inside the coalmine; it crossed a bog and used an aqueduct over the River Irwell. He had no large earth-moving machinery: it was all done by labourers with shovels and wheelbarrows. As they were working with boats they came to be called 'navigators', or navvies. Source 12 describes other ideas of Brindley's.

The smith's forges, the carpenter's and mason's workshops were covered and floated in the canal, following the work from place to place. The Duke made the rubbish of one place help to build another. Thus the stones which were dug up to form the basin for the boats at Worsley were cut into different shapes to build bridges or the arches of the AQUEDUCT. The clay, gravel and earth taken up to preserve the level at one place were carried down the canal to raise the land in another.

SOURCE 12
A description of Brindley's work, written in 1793.

SOURCE 13
Pont Cysyllte designed by Thomas Telford, carrying the canal 127 feet (39m) above the River Dee.

'Cottages are now covered with tiles or slates from Wales or Cumberland. Fields are now drained, manured and covered with a beautiful greenness. Places which rarely knew the use of coal are plentifully supplied with it at reasonable prices. Communication being opened between Liverpool, Bristol and Hull brings in corn in a way unknown in the past.'

SOURCE 14
Benefits of the canals, as described in 1782.

Canals and industry

The canal did exactly what the Duke had hoped: the price of his coal in Manchester fell from 3p to 1½p per hundredweight (50kg). Source 12 also tells us how people marvelled at Brindley's work. Soon other canals were built. The Bridgewater Canal was extended to Liverpool. The 'grand cross' of canals linked the great rivers of Severn, Mersey, Trent and Thames. The Midlands benefited from these links. Josiah Wedgwood built his new factory at Etruria next to the Trent and Mersey Canal (see page 21). His freight charges from Etruria to Manchester dropped from £2.75 to 75p per ton.

There was then a lull in canal building until 1791–1794 when several more were built. The early canals were narrow and winding as they avoided having too many locks. Later canals were wider and the builders used flights of locks, tunnels and huge aqueducts to cross hills and valleys (see Source 13). For all of the early years of the Industrial Revolution, from the 1770s to the 1840s, canals were the main means of transport. Source 14 describes the benefits of canals as seen at the time. In addition to industrial products, especially coal, canals carried iron ore, bricks, timber, clay and fertiliser. Some barges were converted to carry animals to market. Many carried passengers: from 1774, for example, a comfortable passenger service ran from Altrincham to Manchester.

As we have seen, the main advantage of canals was that they were cheap. They were also very slow, and a heavy frost or long drought could bring the whole system to a halt. Long-distance journeys were also difficult because different canals were owned by different companies; this led to delays and expense.

Canal families

There were 25,000 canal barges in 1850, employing about 50,000 people. In the early years boatpeople had homes on land. From the 1840s railways were in fierce competition with canals. Wages were cut and families had to abandon their homes and live on the barge. They had the most cramped living conditions in the country. They cooked, ate and slept in a tiny cabin at the stern of the barge. All the family helped to operate the boat, but only the man was paid. Hours were long and children had little time for school or play (see Sources 15, 16 and 17).

SOURCE 15
Photograph of a boatman and his family.

SOURCE 16
19th century picture of canal life.

'I was born on a canal boat. I was never educated, never went to school. I pulled at the rope on the towpath when I were a baby almost. The canal and the boat and the rope have been my mates always. I married a boat girl, a real woman she was in her way, stronger than a horse. I have three sons and two daughters on the canals of England somewhere, married and with children.'

SOURCE 17
An old canal boatman describes his life.

ACTIVITY

Working in groups, prepare the script for a TV (or radio) programme to be called 'The Romance of Canals'. Use Sources 15, 16 and 17. Try to tell the truth about canal life. Decide what pictures to show and what commentary will be needed. Include interviews with all the people in Source 16.

Railways: fast and cheap

Several inventions came together to create the age of railways. One was the discovery that horses could pull quite heavy loads on rails; the best rails were iron plates, so they were called plateways (see Source 18). There were about 300 miles of plateways in Britain by 1810, mainly in the coalfields along the River Tyne.

We have seen (pages 14–15) that early steam-engines were enormous. What was needed was one small enough to go on rails but strong enough to pull wagons. The first LOCOMOTIVE to do this was built by Richard Trevithick in South Wales in 1804. By 1823, 20 similar locomotives were put to use in the Tyneside coalfields. George Stephenson became skilled in designing, building and driving these locomotives and railways.

A Quaker businessman, Edward Pease, asked Stephenson to design a much longer line. It would go from the coalmines near Darlington, 40 kilometres to the port of Stockton-on-Tees. The railway opened in 1825 and was a great success. It used horses, locomotives and steam-engines. Stephenson compared all three and showed that locomotives were 30 per cent cheaper. His 'Locomotion No. 1' (see Source 19) could pull 75 tonnes of coal at a steady 8 kph.

Business people in Liverpool and Manchester were dissatisfied with the canal link between the two cities. The success of the Stockton and Darlington Railway led them to plan a railway. Stephenson laid out the line and then won a competition, with his famous 'Rocket', to provide the locomotives for it. The line was opened in 1830 and made good profits from the beginning.

SOURCE 18
Horse-drawn coal wagon on a plateway, 1764.

This was followed by a huge amount of railway building: nearly 3,200 kilometres were finished by 1842, over 11,000 by 1852 and the network covered over 33,000 kilometres by 1892. All major cities and industrial areas were linked. At its peak, nearly 7 per cent of Britain's income was being invested in building new railways.

Not all this building was well planned. The government did not think it was its job to interfere. There were 104 different railway companies in 1844. Several lines were built linking the same places. Most railways were built to George Stephenson's 4 feet 8½ inch (143 cm) gauge, but in the west of England Brunel built on the grand 7 feet (213 cm) gauge. All this meant that railways in Britain cost more than railways in other countries to build.

SOURCE 19
Modern replica of Stephenson's 'Locomotion No. 1'.

Navvies

The actual work of building the lines was done by gangs of navvies. There were perhaps 250,000 of them at the peak of building in 1847. They were paid high wages, up to 15p a day; in return they were expected to shovel about 10 tonnes of earth each. Conditions of work were often dangerous too (see Source 20). It is small wonder that they had a terrible reputation (see Source 21).

Impact of railways on industry

Firstly, all industry found that railways provided fast, cheap transport for all kinds of goods from bulky raw materials to expensive manufactured items. The whole economy benefited.

Secondly, the railways themselves used enormous quantities of iron and steel for rails, locomotives, signals, trucks and buildings. The demand for iron and steel increased by about 25 per cent. In addition there was a huge demand for bricks for cuttings, bridges and buildings and timber for sleepers and carriages. Locomotives made new demands for coal: about a tonne per 160 kilometres each.

Thirdly, apart from navvies, there were lots of jobs on the railways: 300,000 of them by 1890.

Finally, the old stagecoach business collapsed fast (see Source 22). Canals declined too, but more slowly.

SOURCE 20
Navvies at work on a cutting for the broad gauge west of England line in 1841.

SOURCE 21
Description of navvies written in 1851.

'Rude, rugged and uncultivated, with great animal strength, collected in large numbers, living and working entirely together, they are a class by themselves. Unable to read and unwilling to be taught, impulsive and brute-like, they live for the present, care not for the past, are indifferent to the future. Insolent and insulting, they are dreaded by the good and welcomed by the bad.'

Before the Liverpool–Manchester railway stagecoaches could carry 688 persons per day. The railway, from its beginning, carried an average of 1,070 per day. The fare by coach was 50p inside and 25p outside; by railway it is 25p inside and 17p outside. The time of the journey by coach was four hours; by railway it is one and three quarter hours. All the coaches but one have ceased running. Goods delivered in Manchester are received the same day in Liverpool; by canal they were never delivered before the third day.

SOURCE 22
Effects of the Liverpool–Manchester railway on coach and canal transport, described in 1832.

1. What is dangerous about the working conditions in Source 20?
2. How would working on a motorway building site today look different?
3. What is the attitude of the author of Source 21 to navvies?
4. How useful is Source 21 to us in finding out about navvies?

How did the railways change people's lives?

Even if you never travelled by train, your life was changed by the railways. There was a wider variety of goods in the shops. Fresh milk, fruit and vegetables from the countryside were brought into towns and cities. Fish could be sent rapidly by rail from ports and sold while it was still fresh. Source 23 describes the effect of the coming of the railway on the town itself. New suburbs were built and city workers began to commute from them (see unit 4). Entirely new towns, such as Crewe, Swindon and Wolverton were built for the railways. More people went on seaside holidays, so seaside towns expanded.

Local variations between different parts of the country were broken down. Before railways, clocks in different towns were faster or slower than each other. Railways introduced standard time everywhere. National newspapers could be printed and sent all over the country; everyone read the same news stories. National political parties and trade unions could be set up (see unit 5). As people from different parts of Britain came into more contact with one another, local accents and dialect became less extreme.

> Roads and bridges that had led to nothing, led to villas, gardens, churches, healthy public walks. There were railway patterns in the draper's shops. There were railway hotels, plans, maps, views; railway buses, railway streets and buildings. There were crowds of people and mountains of goods departing and arriving scores of times every day.

SOURCE 23
From the novel *Dombey and Son* by Charles Dickens, published in 1848.

What was it like to travel by train?

The builders of the first railways expected them to carry mainly goods. In fact, from the first, passengers flocked to travel on them. The Liverpool–Manchester Railway carried 445,000 people in its first year. By 1897 over 11 million passenger journeys were made per year.

Nor were all these passengers rich by any means. By the 1840s working people wanted to be on the move: leaving home, finding jobs, visiting relatives. Source 24 shows the huge variety of the travelling public. Cheap excursions attracted people to take a day out and see places they had never seen before (Source 25). Some railway companies did not encourage lower-class travel at all and offered only the most basic coaches. Travel in such open coaches

SOURCE 24
Paddington Station, London – a painting by William Frith, 1862.

SOURCE 25
Poster advertising railway excursion trips to Blackpool, 1850.

'Sparks flew over us in some quantity. One burnt Miss de Ros's cheek, another a hole in Maria's silk cloak and a third in someone else's gown. The only casualty, apart from several hats being blown away, was a gentleman who got up from his seat before the train came to a stop. He fell overboard.'

SOURCE 26
Some dangers of travelling by train in the 1840s.

could be quite hazardous (Source 26). At the same time coaches for first-class passengers were luxurious (Source 27).

By the end of the 19th century fast, comfortable trains were available to all. Express trains averaged over 100 kph. From 1875 even third-class passengers had padded seats (Source 28). There were restaurant cars, heating, lighting, lavatories and sleeping cars.

SOURCE 27
First-class dining car, 1888.

SOURCE 28
Third-class compartment on a train on the Midland Railway.

attainment target 3

1. What do the sources on these pages tell us about what it was like to travel by train?
2. What do Sources 25, 27 and 28 tell us about differences between classes in 19th century Britain?
3. Which sources here are most useful for finding out about:
   What rail travel was like?
   How people felt about rail travel?
4. Source 23 is from a novel; Source 24 is a painting. How reliable will the evidence from them be?
5. What kinds of evidence can we get from Sources 23 and 24 even though they are both works of art?

UNIT 4

AIMS

The number of people in Britain increased rapidly in the period 1750–1900. In this unit we shall see why, and how the extra people were fed. We shall also see that more and more people in Britain went to live in cities.

In unit 1 we looked at people's working lives. In this unit we will look at what it was like to live in a 19th century city. We will compare city life with country life and decide which was better.

Living in cities

The crowded scene in Source 1 was not unusual at that time. Everyone lent a hand with the harvest and there were plenty of people in the countryside to help. At the time the picture was painted, four out of every five people in Britain lived in rural areas. Over the next 170 years great changes came over the population of Britain: the number of people increased enormously and the balance between country and city was reversed. The crowded city street in Source 2 could not have been drawn in 1750. By 1850 such scenes were common.

SOURCE 1
Harvesting in Gloucestershire, about 1730.

SOURCE 2
Traffic jam in mid-19th century London.

Population rise

We have no accurate figures for the population of Britain before 1801. Since then a CENSUS has been made every ten years. Historians make estimates for the years before 1801. Their estimate for Britain in 1750 is about 10.7 million. Source 3 shows that the population then rose steeply. In fact, it was the fastest population rise in the history of Britain: it rose by at least 10 per cent every ten years from 1780 to 1911. From 1811 to 1821 it rose by 17 per cent. Nowadays the rise is nearer 4 per cent every ten years.

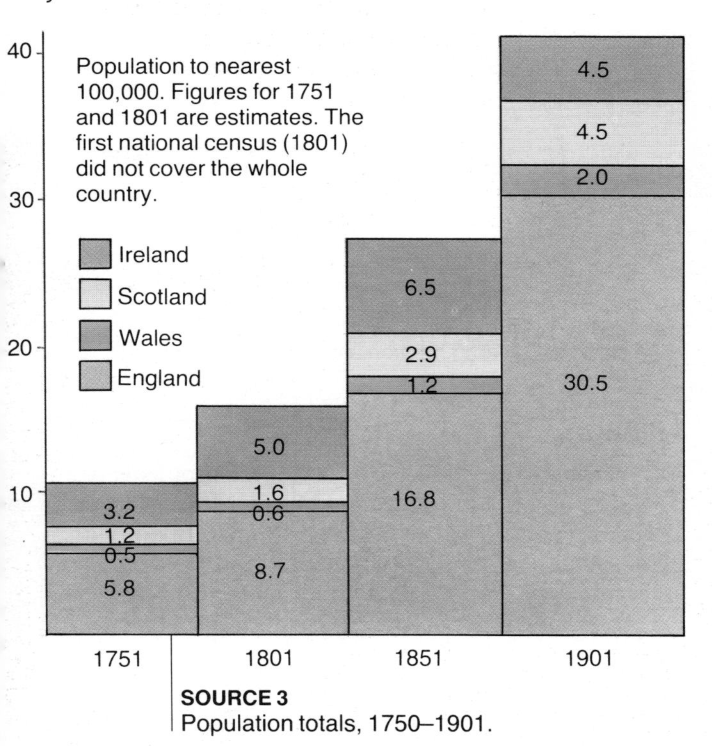

SOURCE 3
Population totals, 1750–1901.

	1750	1851
London	657,000	2,491,000
Liverpool	22,000	376,000
Glasgow	23,000	345,000
Manchester	18,000	303,000
Birmingham	24,000	233,000
Leeds	10,000	172,000
Bristol	50,000	137,000
Newcastle	28,000	88,000
Preston	5,000	70,000
Norwich	35,000	68,000
Brighton	5,000	66,000

SOURCE 4
Town growth, 1750–1851.

Why did the population rise?

There are only three possible answers: more people came to live here; fewer people died; more people were born.

People did move to Britain, but many EMIGRATED (see page 76) so that cannot be the reason. Nor did death become less common. As we shall see in this unit, killer diseases took their toll throughout this period. It is possible that people were better fed (see page 52) so more resistant to illness, but that was only a minor factor.

The main factor seems to be that more people married and married younger. The number of unmarried people fell from 15 per cent to 7 per cent of the population. The average age of marriage fell from about 27 to about 24. These changes led to more babies being born.

Why did these changes happen?

One reason was that there were better harvests in the 18th century, so food was cheaper. Wages went further and people could afford to get married. However, the main reason was that men and women, particularly young people, were moving to towns to work in industry. They could earn good wages and were free to make their own decisions. Back home, parents might interfere; many farming jobs meant living in the farmer's house as a single person. Factory-owners took no such interest in their employees' personal lives. In fact, the average age of marriage in industrial areas was nearer 20. Married couples in industrial cities may have chosen to have big families as children could earn money working in the factories (see page 23).

The results of this move to the cities can be seen in Source 4. From 1750 to 1851 the population of rural Britain rose by 88 per cent; the population of urban areas rose by 129 per cent. Many of the places listed grew even faster than that. By 1851, for the first time, more British people lived in URBAN areas than in the countryside.

Discuss your ideas about these questions in pairs.

1. Why were cities attractive to young people?
2. How do you think the increase in the number of people would affect:
   the need for food?
   the demand for goods such as clothing?
3. Did the population rise cause the growth of cities, or did the growth of cities cause the rise in population?

How were these people fed?

The population of Britain doubled in the century up to 1851. How were all these people fed? The answer lies in changes in farming methods. Farming before the 18th century was locked into a system of low yields. There was no way of FERTILISING the land except by the manure of animals. Crops such as wheat and barley were grown for two years on the same land, by which time it was exhausted. It was then left fallow (no crop was grown) while the animals grazed on it, fertilising it with their droppings. This system, called a three-CROP ROTATION, had been used across much of England for centuries. It meant that one third of the land was lying idle every year; farmers could not grow more crops because the land was exhausted; they could not keep more animals because they had no FODDER for them.

Back in the mid-17th century, many Royalists fled abroad to Holland after the Civil War. They saw that Dutch farmers grew turnips as fodder for animals. When they returned to Britain in 1660, some landowners tried this system. They used a four-crop rotation (see Source 5). More fodder meant that more animals could be kept, so there was more manure. More manure improved the fertility of the soil and better crops could be grown.

While all the animals grazed together on the fallow field or on the common, they interbred and were usually thin and diseased. Farmers began to try to improve the quality of their animals by 'selective breeding'; that is, breeding carefully from selected animals to produce certain features such as more meat or better wool. An example of the results can be seen in Source 6. The average weight of cattle sold at Smithfield market in London rose from 145 kg in 1710 to 363 kg in 1795; the average weight of sheep rose from 13 kg to 36 kg in the same period.

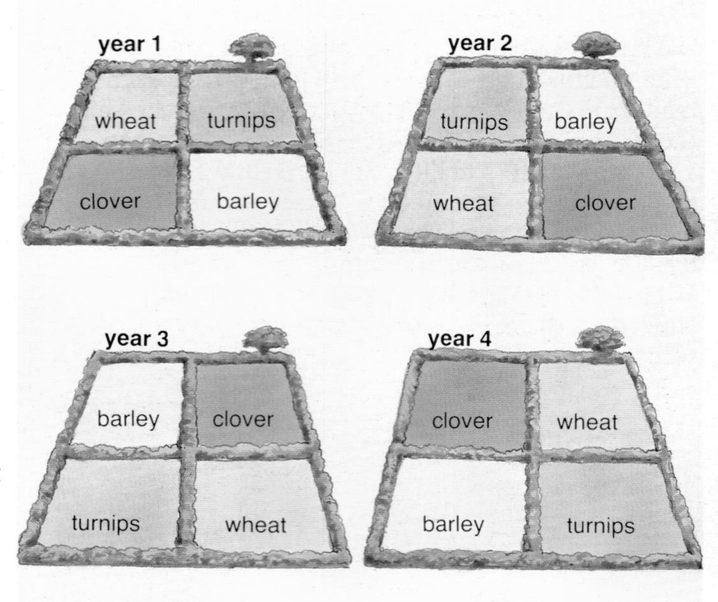

SOURCE 5
The Norfolk four-crop rotation system.

Enclosure

One of the main obstacles to better farming was the way much of the land was organised. Many villages in central and southern England still had open fields. (You will have found out about this when you were studying *Medieval Realms*.) It was hard to introduce new crops or breed better animals in the OPEN FIELD system. It was not worth improving your own land, for example by draining it. Everyone had to work together because their STRIPS were scattered across the open fields. Enclosure simply means dividing open land into small fields and putting hedges round them. Everyone then had their own fields and could use them as they wished. Source 7 shows some land enclosed in 1795. The hedges mark out the fields but the old strips of the open fields can still be seen.

Sometimes villagers agreed to enclose their open fields. Other open land such as commons and greens could also be enclosed in this way. If they did not agree, then the owners of four fifths of the land could force through enclosure by Act of Parliament. There was a great increase in the number of Enclosure Acts passed in the 18th century, from about 30 a year to over 60. From 1801 to 1810 there were 906. In all, nearly 3 million hectares of land were enclosed.

SOURCE 6
Prize bulls of improved breeds with their herdsmen.

SOURCE 7
Aerial photograph showing enclosure hedges of 1795 lying across the old open field strips.

SOURCE 8
Thomas Coke at Holkham, Norfolk.

a 'Turnips were common over most of the eastern and southern parts of England by the reign of Queen Anne.' (Queen Anne died in 1714.)

b 'In 1730 it was an extensive heath without tree or shrub. Now in 1780 the whole is laid out in the Norfolk system and let at 75p an acre, ten times its original value.'

c 'The present pre-eminence of the county in improved agriculture is due alone to the celebrated Coke of Norfolk.'

SOURCE 9
Some views of Thomas Coke (from the top): Daniel Defoe, 1724; Arthur Young, 1780; James Caird, 1850.

Who benefited?

It was the better-off farmers and landowners who gained most. Enclosure was expensive. It cost money to pass an Act of Parliament. Then there was the cost of mapping the land and dividing it up. The new fields had to be hedged. Only those who had money to start with could afford it. Poorer farmers lost out. SMALLHOLDERS who had lived for years on common land but did not have a written title to their holding might end up with nothing. The agricultural writer Arthur Young encouraged all forms of improvement but was horrified at some of the results of enclosure. One farm labourer told him: 'All I know is that I had a cow and an Act of Parliament has taken it from me.' There were riots in some villages.

Spreading ideas

All these new ideas took time to spread. Some landowners became famous as improvers. One was Viscount Townshend. He popularised the growing of turnips in Norfolk in the 1730s. Even more famous was Sir Thomas Coke, who farmed at Holkham in north Norfolk from 1776 to 1842. As many as 7,000 people used to come to his 'sheep shearings' (Source 8). Farmers and dukes would meet there and compare ideas. The three extracts in Source 9 help you to examine Coke's reputation.

Results

Changing British farming was a long, slow process. Unlike industry, which we looked at in unit 1, agricultural improvement before 1850 did not mean using machines. The number of people working in agriculture rose from 1.7 million in 1801 to 2.1 million in 1851. However, as we have seen, the population rose much faster than this.

Workers were thus available for industry. The result of the improvements was that all those extra mouths could be fed, and fed cheaply. Cheap food meant that industrial wages did not have to be high, which pleased industrialists.

1 Which of the three statements in Source 9 shows most admiration for Coke?

2 In what ways might statements **a** and **b** contradict statement **c**?

3 Why is Viscount Townshend important?

The walking city

SOURCE 10
Sheffield in about 1850.

The rise in the population of Britain was described on page 50. Before 1851, most of these people were born in the countryside. Improvements in farming brought some new jobs, but not enough. Farming wages were low and irregular. The new factories and workshops created by the Industrial Revolution needed thousands of workers. The move to the cities became a flood.

At first people did not move far: perhaps 10–15 miles to the nearest town. But they were mainly young, and felt free to move on again if better prospects turned up elsewhere. They were joined by people from other parts of Britain, Ireland and the rest of Europe. Teeming masses of people, most of them born in the country, caused cities in the early 19th century to grow rapidly.

Cities at this time had no public transport to speak of. People had to live within walking distance of their work. This produced the close-packed landscape of houses, factories, shops and churches you can see in Source 10. This was called 'the walking city'. Workers woke to the sound of the factory bell or hooter. Their houses were blackened by smoke from factory chimneys.

Housing

With so many people wanting to live and work in cities, housing was in great demand. Large, old houses were split up, with families sharing a flat or even a room. Builders realised that there were profits to be made from building cheap houses quickly. Thousands of small houses were built in this way, usually in TERRACES.

SOURCE 11
Back-to-back houses near Halifax, Yorkshire.

SOURCE 12
Houses with separate cellar-dwellings in Merthyr Tydfil, Wales.

'Most of those districts lived in by the millworkers are newly built. The houses are ill-drained, often ill-ventilated, unprovided with toilets. As a result, the streets, which are narrow, become the resting place of mud, refuse and disgusting rubbish. In Parliament Street there is one toilet for 380 inhabitants.'

SOURCE 13
Description of Manchester in 1832.

Source 11 shows a common way of getting a lot of houses into the space available: back-to-back. Source 12 shows another way of cramming in more families. In 1840, a government report found 15,000 people in Manchester and 39,000 in Liverpool living in one-room cellars. Sources 13 and 14 describe some of the results of this overcrowding.

Health

Overcrowding was just one side of a serious health problem in cities. At that time no one understood the need for clean water, good drainage, SEWAGE systems and refuse disposal. There were no planning laws.

Water was often not piped to poor people's houses. It had to be bought from water-carriers or carried from standpipes in the street. Drains and sewers were not provided either and there was no system of refuse disposal. Dirty water, sewage and rubbish therefore piled up in the streets or in overflowing pits.

The effects of this situation on health can be seen in Source 15. Cities were obviously very unhealthy places. Children and babies were most at risk: the death rate of working-class under-fives in Preston in 1851 was 63 per 1,000. In Britain today it is 16 per 1,000.

'Between the backyards of the two rows of cottages, a cesspool extends the whole length of the street which receives the contents of the privies [lavatories] and drains . . . The contents of the cesspool belong to the landlord and are taken out twice a year.'

SOURCE 14
Description of cottages in Preston, Lancashire, in 1844.

	Wiltshire	Liverpool
Gentry, professional people and their families	50	35
Farmers, tradesmen and their families	48	22
Labourers and their families	33	15

SOURCE 15
Average ages of death, 1842.

ACTIVITY

Work in groups of four. Using the information and sources on these pages, put together a report on living conditions in 19th century towns. In your report, you can write up interviews with eye-witnesses who saw what conditions were like, as well as adding notes and sketches of your own. The final report can be in the form of a booklet, to be sent to the government to demand some improvement.

Look at Source 15.

1 What do these statistics tell us?
2 Suggest reasons for the differences between the figures for Wiltshire and Liverpool.
3 Suggest reasons for the differences between the figures for the different classes.
4 Why do you think the government allowed houses like those in Sources 11 and 12 to be built?

Housing and health

In the walking city the demand for somewhere to live was high. Some people could only afford to rent a room, or half a room, or only a bed or, at the worst, part of a bed. Of 1,462 families surveyed in one parish in London, half only had one bed for the entire family.

Typhus, carried by lice, tuberculosis, transmitted from one person's breath to another, and typhoid, spread by drinking polluted water, flourished in these conditions. Source 16 shows the kind of overcrowding still to be found in 1900.

The disease which really made people aware of conditions in cities was cholera. This was a disease new to Britain. It brought sickness, vomiting, diarrhoea and rapid death. In a few months in 1831–1832 32,000 people died. It was followed by further EPIDEMICS in 1848 and 1865–1866. Doctors pointed out the link between bad housing and numerous deaths from cholera (see Source 17).

Ignorance of basic hygiene made matters worse, as Source 18 shows.

SOURCE 16
Street in Glasgow, 1900.

> On 26 May the first case of pure cholera occurred in Blue Bell Fold, a small, dirty cul-de-sac containing about 20 houses inhabited by poor families. It lies between the river and an offensive streamlet which carries refuse water from numerous mills and dyehouses.
>
> The first case occurred in a child, two years of age, in perfect health on the preceding day, who became suddenly ill on the morning of the 26th and died at 5 p.m. on the same day.

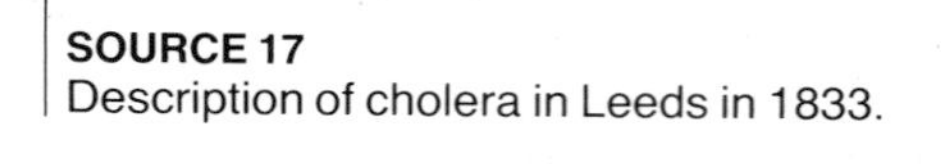

SOURCE 17
Description of cholera in Leeds in 1833.

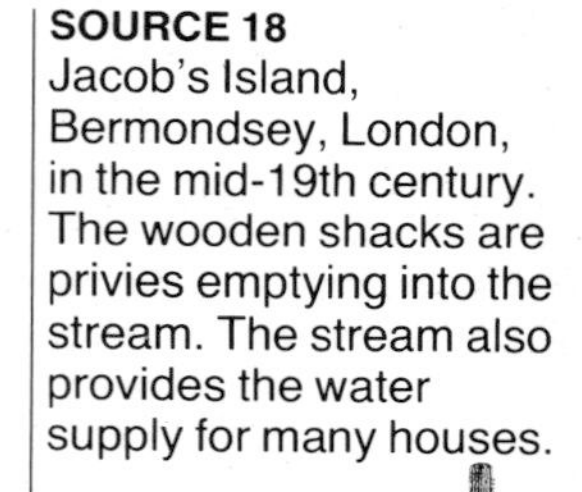

SOURCE 18
Jacob's Island, Bermondsey, London, in the mid-19th century. The wooden shacks are privies emptying into the stream. The stream also provides the water supply for many houses.

Urban life

Today several museums try to show what 19th century urban life was like. Sources 19, 20 and 21 are photographs from a modern museum.

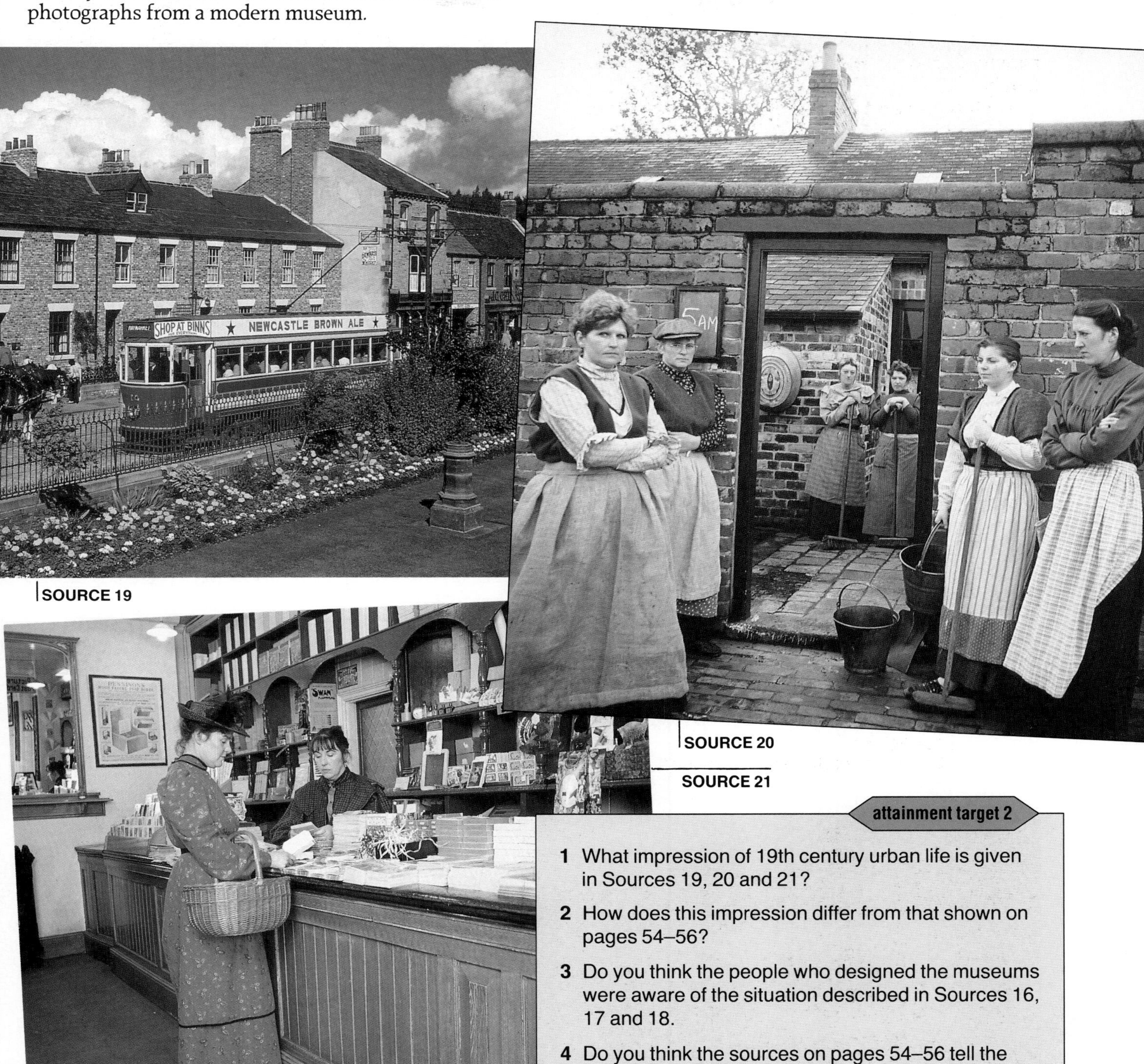

SOURCE 19

SOURCE 20

SOURCE 21

attainment target 2

1. What impression of 19th century urban life is given in Sources 19, 20 and 21?
2. How does this impression differ from that shown on pages 54–56?
3. Do you think the people who designed the museums were aware of the situation described in Sources 16, 17 and 18.
4. Do you think the sources on pages 54–56 tell the whole story?
5. Which of the two interpretations of city life do you think is:
   a more popular?
   b more truthful?

Country life: dream or reality?

A factory workers' song, called 'The Factory Bell', envied the life of the farm worker:

> 'Oh happy man, oh happy thou,
> While toiling at thy spade and plough,
> Here at the mills in pressing crowds
> The high-built chimneys puff black clouds
> And all around the slaves do dwell
> Who're called to labour by a bell.'

We have seen that factory work and city life in the early 19th century were pretty grim. Was the life of country people at this time as happy as the song says? Source 22 paints a cosy picture of rural life. The rest of the sources will help you to make up your own mind.

SOURCE 22
Country cottage, as painted by Helen Allingham in the late 19th century.

Housing

The houses farm labourers lived in were often just as bad as the conditions in cities described on pages 54–56. Usually they were 'tied cottages'. That is, they belonged to the farmers who rented them to their labourers. Farmers were reluctant to spend money improving them and they were often unhygienic and overcrowded. The cartoon (Source 23) complains that the farmer pays more attention to the stables for his horses than the cottage for his labourers. Source 24 shows how hard women's lives could be in this situation.

SOURCE 23
Cartoon from *Punch*, 1861. The squire, at the door, is being told: 'Your stables are excellent! Suppose you try something like that here, eh?'

SOURCE 24
Washing day – villagers are washing clothes in the stream, using wooden tubs. Probably their cottages did not have running water.

Work and wages

Farm machinery only began to be used on a large scale in the later 19th century, so until then there was plenty of work on the land. However there were plenty of people looking for work too, so wages were low. Source 25 shows how difficult it was for farm labourers to live.

Jobs such as the harvest (Source 26) could be fun, but the work itself was hard, with long hours. There were few jobs to be done in the winter and labourers were often laid off then. All the family had to work to help make ends meet, as Source 27 explains. Women were paid less than men, and children often only 6d (2½p) a week.

Freedom and control

If a farm labourer in a tied cottage lost his job, he and his family lost their home as well. This meant that people did not dare to complain about anything. The SQUIRE, the PARSON and the farmers were more than just employers: they expected labourers and their families to look up to them at all times. The parson's wife described in Source 28 might have some money or clothes to hand out, but only to those she thought deserved them. This explains the attitude of the women in the source.

Wages

Husband 8 shillings; wife 6d; Total 8s 6d [42½p]

Expenses	
Flour for bread, 7½ gallons	6s 3d
Yeast	2½d
Salt	1½d
Bacon: 1 lb, boiled with vegetables	8d
Tea 1 oz	2d
Sugar 4 oz	6d
Butter 8 oz	4d
Soap 4 oz	2¼d
Candles 5 oz	3d
Thread for mending clothes	3d
Total	8s 11¼d [45p]

SOURCE 25
Weekly budget of a farm labourer's family, early 18th century.

SOURCE 26
Break for lunch during the hay harvest.

'On the day that I was eight years of age I left school and began to work 14 hours a day in the fields with 40 or 50 children of whom I was the eldest. We were followed all day long by an old man carrying a long whip in his hand which he did not forget to use. A great many of the children were only five years old.'

SOURCE 27
A woman, over 80 years old, remembers working as a girl in the 1850s.

'The Parson's wife used to sit in state in her pew in the church and the poor women used to walk up the church and make a curtsey to her before taking the seats set apart for them.'

SOURCE 28
Description of attitudes in a Warwickshire village in the 1830s.

attainment target 2

1. Give one fact and one opinion from the sources and text on these pages.
2. Helen Allingham painted the cottage in Source 22 while looking at it; do you think the painting is an expression of fact or opinion?
3. In what ways was country life not the dream which Source 22 portrays?
4. Which of Sources 23–28 supports the idea that people were happier in the countryside? Which of the sources contradicts that idea?
5. Why do you think many people in the 19th century thought that country life was better than city life?
6. Why do you think many people still think that today?

The changing city: suburbs

Public transport

By the later 19th century better public transport was putting an end to 'the walking city'. There were horse-drawn buses in Manchester from 1824. Horse-drawn trams were introduced in 1860 and electric trams from 1885. By 1914 there were 2,500 miles of tram routes in British cities, providing cheap transport for millions. Railway companies bought land beside rail routes and built houses on it, encouraging people to move out of the city. Some ran 'workmen's specials' with cheap tickets for working people on early morning trains. In London the working-class suburb of Willesden rose in population from 3,000 in 1851 to 114,000 in 1891. West Ham's population rose from 19,000 to 267,000 over the same period.

Source 29 describes the growth of different suburbs for different kinds of middle-class commuters. The horse-drawn bus in Source 30 would take you into central London for one penny. So began the process of moving out of the city, which has been going on ever since.

> The railways have set us all moving far away from London – that is to say the middle class of Londoners, people ranging from three to five hundred a year. They betake themselves to far-off spots like Richmond, Watford, Croydon or Slough. The smaller fry content themselves with semi-detached boxes at Putney, Kilburn, New Cross or Ealing but the wealthier are found to go daily to the capital from as far as Reading or Brighton.

SOURCE 29
Description of the growth of London's suburbs, written in 1873.

SOURCE 30
Horse-drawn bus in a suburban road in north London.

SOURCE 31
Interior of a Victorian house. Typical features are the tiles, plantpot, oriental carpet and heavy drapes.

Suburban houses

There was space in the suburbs to build large detached or semi-detached houses for middle-class commuters. These were sometimes called villas. Builders were helped by the advances of the Industrial Revolution. Bricks and glass could now be produced cheaply in large quantities in factories, rather than by hand. Welsh or Cornish roofing slates could be brought cheaply by rail.

Source 31 shows what the inside of a Victorian villa was like. Industrial Britain was prosperous and the middle classes had money to spend on making their houses fashionable. Factory-made tiles, stained glass, mirrors, ornaments, curtains and heavy furniture were reasonably priced. British trading links across the world (see unit 2) brought all kinds of goods from abroad, such as the eastern carpet in Source 31, brass from India, mahogany from Africa and so on. People could live at a standard of luxury which only the rich could have afforded a hundred years earlier. As we have seen, servants were cheap (see page 25) so cleaning and dusting masses of ornaments was not a problem for them.

William Morris hated factory-made goods and admired eastern designs. He wanted to return to hand-made processes. His own designs for curtains, wallpaper and fabrics are still popular today (see Source 32).

Owners of these suburban villas expected them to include the latest in hygienic inventions, too. Source 33 shows a selection of flush toilets, made in the factories of 'the Potteries'. Their glazed finish meant that germs, unknown before 1861, could be kept at bay.

For those who lived there, the suburbs were pleasant, leafy, quiet places to live. Nineteenth century suburban villas were planned with large gardens, ideal for the friendly tennis party shown in Source 34.

SOURCE 32
Wallpaper designed by William Morris.

SOURCE 33
Museum display of flush toilets.

1 Suggest reasons why middle-class Victorians preferred living in the suburbs.
2 Why was a good public transport system essential for the growth of suburbs?
3 What items which were probably made in a factory can you see in Sources 31, 33 and 34?
4 Do you live in a suburb? What are the advantages and disadvantages of living there?

SOURCE 34
Painting of a tennis party in the garden of a middle-class villa in Leamington.

Changing cities: the City Fathers

We have seen that early 19th century cities sprang up with no planning or controls. This was not because local councils did not care what happened; it was because they believed it was not their job to interfere in things like housing or hygiene. They thought that governments only make things worse and that people will sort things out for the best, on their own. This was called '**laissez-faire**' and some ideas about what governments should and should not do can be seen in Source 35.

> 'What are the duties of the government? To restrain crime, to protect property, to pass laws to protect order and justice, to conduct relations with other countries.
>
> It is not the duty of government to feed or clothe people, to build houses for them, to regulate their work or their families, or supply them with teachers, doctors or books.'

SOURCE 35
'Laissez-faire', as explained by Edward Baines in a letter written in 1846.

Municipal Corporations Act, 1835

Many cities had grown so fast that they hardly had any local government. Some towns had local councils, called corporations, but they were often not elected and usually did very little. The Municipal Corporations Act of 1835 set up new corporations in 178 towns or cities. By 1903 another 135 towns or cities had gained the same rights. These included places as large as Birmingham, Manchester, Huddersfield, Bradford, Halifax and Rochdale.

These new corporations were intended to be more democratic, following the changes made to Parliamentary voting by the 1832 Reform Act (see page 73). In fact, only better-off males could vote at first, about 5 per cent of the adult population. Later in the century, the right to vote was widened. The new corporations also had few powers at first. Many things which local councils do now, such as street cleaning and lighting, were still looked after by other people.

SOURCE 36
Sewers being built in London, 1862.

However, as the 19th century went on, it became clear that 'laissez-faire' was not providing answers to the terrible problems of the cities. The middle-class voters who controlled the new corporations wanted to take action. Gradually, their powers were increased. This was the great age of city corporations. Joseph Chamberlain, Mayor of Birmingham 1873–1876, carried out several improvements in the city. Led by him, the city bought up and demolished 16 hectares (40 acres) of slums near the city centre and built impressive new roads. This kind of bold action was the opposite of 'laissez-faire' and gained the name 'MUNICIPAL SOCIALISM'.

City corporations could raise money from local taxes, called rates. They were not afraid to spend to solve their problems. Health was a major concern, and many towns spent heavily on putting in drains, sewers and a good water supply. From 1860 to 1900 Bradford spent £1.5 million on street improvement, £300,000 on drains and £3 million on the water supply. Source 36 shows new sewers being built in London.

To the 'City Fathers', as the councillors were often called, health meant fresh air too. Rapidly growing, unplanned cities had few open spaces for the public. Municipal parks, with flowerbeds, paths, seats, a boating lake and a bandstand were provided in many cities (see Source 37). The rising population meant that the old graveyards became full. New municipal cemeteries were laid out on the edge of the city. Municipal baths and wash-houses were built, too.

SOURCE 37
Bandstand in the People's Park, Halifax, Yorkshire.

SOURCE 38
Inside the Market Hall, Bolton, Lancashire.

The City Fathers were proud of their city and wanted buildings to be proud of. In many northern cities the corporation controlled the market and built new market halls (see Source 38). They also wanted the city to be more than just a place of business and industry. City art galleries, museums, libraries, concert halls and lecture rooms were built.

At the centre of it all was a new town hall. It had to have offices for the people running all the new things the city was taking on, a chamber for council meetings, and a grand hall for concerts, dances and lectures. Its architecture also had to express the pride people were beginning to take in their city (see Source 39).

SOURCE 39
Painting of Rochdale Town Hall.

ACTIVITY

1. Get into groups of four. You are councillors in a city in the north of England in 1876.
   Councillor Accrington supports 'laissez-faire' and wants to keep the rates down.
   Councillor Bacup is keen on parks and sport.
   Councillor Congleton feels that the council's priority should be better drains and cleaner streets.
   Councillor Dewsbury wants to offer the people of the town more culture by building an art gallery and buying modern pictures for it.
   Discuss what each of you wants for the town and try to reach a decision.
2. There is to be a grand opening of the new park by the Mayor, with bands, a circus and free ice-cream for the children. Design a poster advertising the event; suggest some of the things the Mayor should say in his speech.

Changing cities: the people

By the end of the 19th century, city life for working people had improved a little. New laws, such as the 1875 Artisans' Dwellings Act, meant that better housing was being built (see Source 40). The improvements to public health described on pages 56–57 brought real benefits. By this time cities had facilities to meet all kinds of interests, from dance halls to chapels.

People joined together in a wide range of clubs and societies. There were 691,410 ALLOTMENTS by 1881. Allotment holders held competitions for chrysanthemums, marrows, leeks. Enthusiasts, usually men, took time and trouble over breeding canaries, pigeons or whippets.

Choirs were very popular, usually as part of church or chapel life (see page 79). Many played in brass bands, often sponsored by a factory-owner. By the end of the century, cycling had become a popular hobby with both sexes.

Thousands began to spend their Saturday afternoons watching sport. Various kinds of football had been popular for centuries. They were crude, rough games, with few rules which varied from place to place. In late 19th century Britain, people were more in touch with each other and a common set of rules was needed. In 1863 the Football Association was formed and agreed the rules. The FA Cup started in 1872. The leaders in this move were upper-class men from public schools. However, football was becoming increasingly popular in working-class northern towns. In 1883 Bolton Olympic beat Old Etonians in the Cup Final and the game changed forever. Big grounds were built in many cities. Fans could travel by train to away matches. Soccer hooliganism began, with attacks on referees and opposing teams.

SOURCE 40
Late 19th century terraces, Manchester. By this time laws had been passed which said that houses had to be a certain distance apart and courtyards had to be open at one end. Compare with Source 16, page 56.

Street life

Many city families were still desperately poor. The children in Source 41 look cheerful but there are signs of their families' poverty. These children, from overcrowded homes, lived on the streets. Source 42 explains how interesting the streets were. Much shopping was still done from market stalls. All kinds of goods were sold from barrows or trays.

There were differences between the sexes in how leisure time was spent. For women, making the money last the week was almost a full-time occupation. A loan from the PAWNSHOP was often the only way of making ends meet. Caring for the children was also mainly women's responsibility. Meeting friends and neighbours in the street helped make these tasks bearable.

SOURCE 41
Children in Liverpool, circa 1900.

First thing in the morning the lamplighter came round with his long pole, turning out the streetlamps and in the evening lighting them again. There were hawkers singing their wares, gypsies to tell your fortune, the cats'meat man with his one-wheel barrow, the milkman ladling milk from a churn on a barrow. Sunday was the day of the muffin man. He came round balancing a large tray on his head, packed with muffins, and ringing a bell, calling out 'Muffins!'. In the afternoon there would be the winkle man calling out from his barrow of winkles, shrimps and cockles. There was a ballad-singer who sang a popular song and sold copies of it for a penny. There was the hurdy-gurdy man, an Italian with a small organ on a short pole and a monkey trained to turn the handle.

SOURCE 42
Childhood memories of Albert Jacobs, born in London in 1889.

SOURCE 43
A city pub: the Falcon, Battersea, London.

Pubs

For men, the most attractive escape from a crowded, shabby house was the pub. With their bright lights, mirrors, polished wooden bars, frosted glass and plush seats they were a little taste of luxury (Source 43). Pubs were the centre of social life, too. Sports teams were run from pubs. Some city pubs had entertainment rooms, which were the origins of the music halls (see Source 44).

Other pubs had meeting rooms for serious occasions. Some Chartists met in pubs (see page 74) and so did some TRADE UNION branches (see page 80). The Hope and Anchor Inn, in Birmingham, had a flourishing debating society. Among the topics they discussed were the abolition of the monarchy, votes for all adults and support for the Midlands miners' strike.

Opposition to pubs came from the powerful TEMPERANCE movement. They blamed alcohol for violence, the breakdown of family life, poverty and the decline of religion. Their attitude to pubs can be read about in Source 45.

SOURCE 44
Acrobats at the Alhambra Music Hall, London.

'Over the door were three enormous lamps. They were in full glare this Sunday evening, and through the doors of these infernal dens of drunkenness and mischief, crowds of miserable wretches were pouring in, that they might drink and die.'

SOURCE 45
A pub as described in a temperance magazine, 1836.

attainment target 1

1. Compare the housing on page 64 with the housing on pages 54–56. What differences can you see?
2. What other differences can you see between city life as described on these pages and on pages 54–56?
3. In what ways does city life seem to have changed least?
4. Use pages 50–65. In what ways did cities seem to have changed most over the 19th century?
5. Which people would find their lives in cities changed most over this period? Which people's lives do you think changed least?

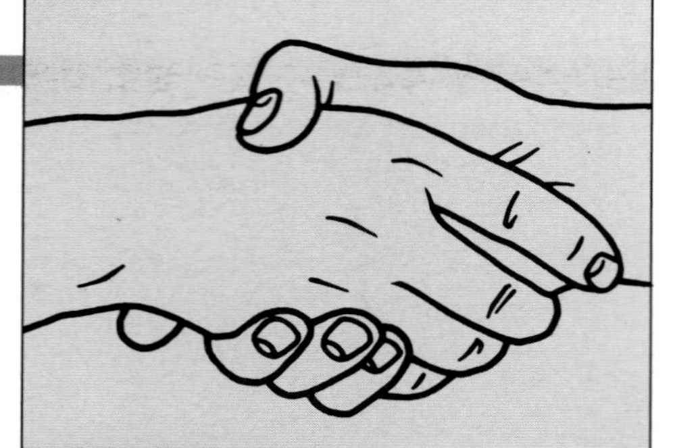

UNIT 5

Popular responses

AIMS

In this unit you will see how the people of Britain reacted to the changes you have read about in other units. Some reacted with violence, some peacefully. Some worked for change through Parliament. Some tried to help themselves through their own actions. As we shall see, some members of the upper and middle classes also tried to improve the situation.

We have seen in this book that changes in industry affected most of the people in Britain, often for the worse. Their working hours were long, hard and sometimes dangerous. Children had to work to make ends meet. Their living conditions were bad. Wages were low and irregular (see Source 1), and could stop altogether if trade was difficult and factories closed. Skilled craftspeople were losing their livelihood as machines took over their work. What could they do about these things?

They certainly could not turn to the government for help. In a modern ELECTION everyone over 18 can vote. Voters can elect people who will do what they think needs doing. The 18th century view of society was that only those who had a stake in the country by owning property should be allowed to vote. Therefore only 4 per cent of adult males, and no women at all, had the right to vote (Source 2).

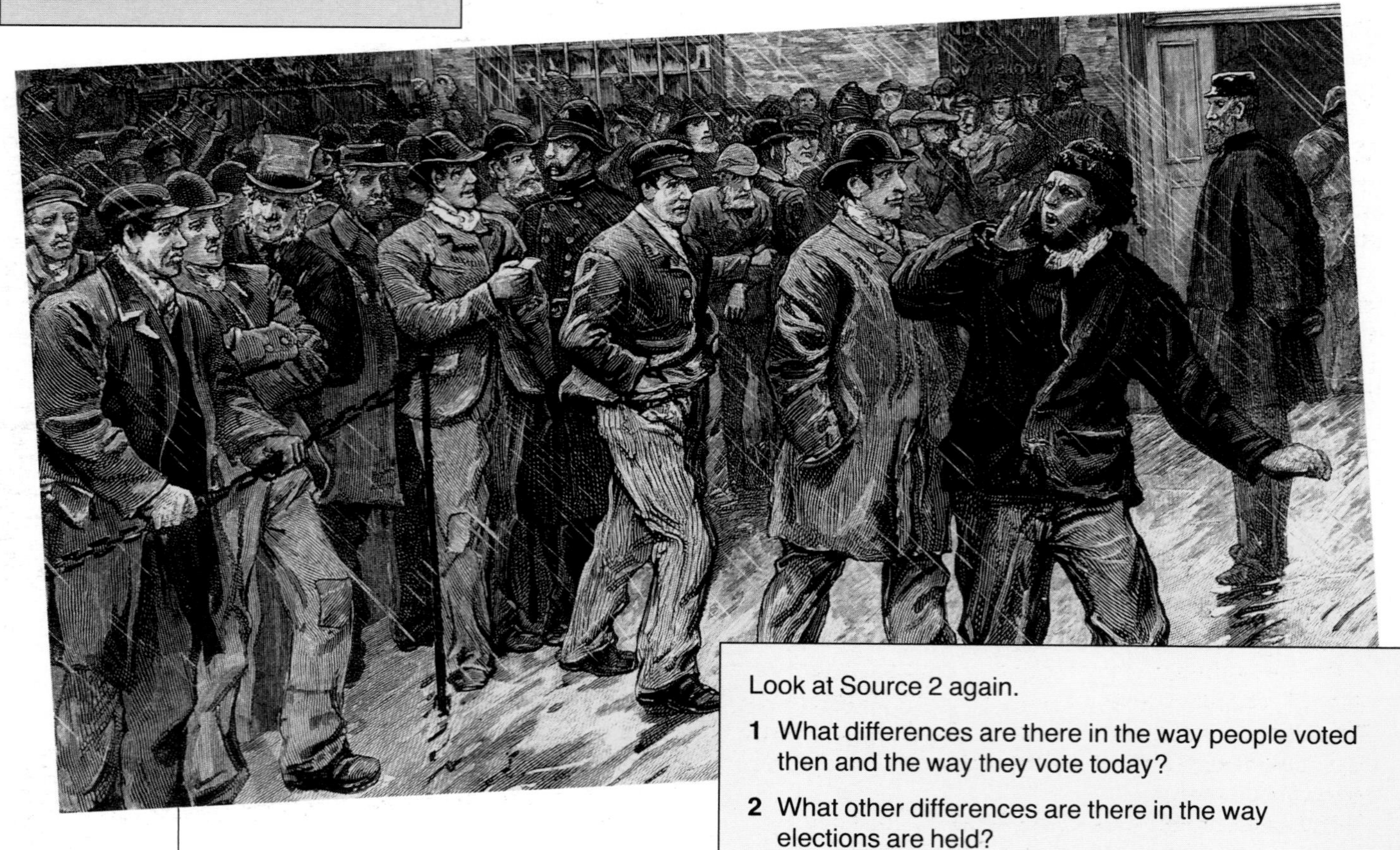

SOURCE 1
Dockers waiting to be chosen for work in London in the 1880s.

Look at Source 2 again.

1 What differences are there in the way people voted then and the way they vote today?

2 What other differences are there in the way elections are held?

3 At the time of Source 2, Members of Parliament had to own property in order to stand for election; they were not paid; elections were held every seven years. What differences are there now?

SOURCE 2
Election scene in Westminster, 1796. The candidates are on a wooden platform (called the hustings), the voters are below. Voting took place in public, over several days. Westminster had an unusually large number of voters.

What could working people do?

Working people were left with only two ways of making their feelings known: peaceful persuasion, by PETITIONS or DEMONSTRATIONS, or violence. This difference in methods runs through this unit.

But what should their targets be? Some wanted to change Parliament, so that it could pass laws to help them (see pages 72 and 74). Some ignored Parliament and put pressure directly on their employers (see page 80). Some worked to make their factories and cities better (also see page 80), while some opted out of the industrial system entirely (see page 76).

The French Revolution

The French Revolution began in 1789. By 1793 the king and hundreds of nobles had been executed. Ideas of 'liberty, equality and fraternity' were being put into practice.

People in Britain were angry enough about the state of their lives to make a revolution possible here. The king was criticised (see Source 3). Corresponding Societies were set up (see Source 4) to write to France to find out more.

The government in Britain was alarmed. They made it clear that no change would take place (see Source 5). Corresponding Societies were banned, printers were imprisoned, newspapers were taxed and trade unions made illegal.

There was no British revolution, but the desire for change could not be crushed so easily.

'A sullen silence hung over the crowd. No hats were pulled off and frequently a cry of "Give us bread!", and once or twice "No King!" with much hissing and groaning.'

SOURCE 3
Crowd reactions to King George III in 1795.

'To show the people the reason for their sufferings: when a man works hard for 14 hours a day, the week through, and is not able to maintain his family.'

SOURCE 4
A witness at the trial of the Secretary of the London Corresponding Society describes the aims of the Society, 1792.

'The British constitution is the best that ever was since the creation of the world and it is not possible to make it any better.'

SOURCE 5
Lord Justice Braxfield's opinion of the British constitution, 1793.

Violent protest

Sometimes people were driven to violence because they were desperate. High food prices and a reduction in wages could mean starving to death and there seemed no peaceful way out.

Who were the Luddites?

Today a Luddite is someone who is against any new machine. In 1811–1812 large groups of workers smashed machines in textile factories in Nottinghamshire, Yorkshire and Lancashire. Twelve thousand troops were sent to these areas to try to keep the peace. The punishments for this kind of thing were serious, so the rioters used a made-up name to protect their leaders: 'Ned Ludd'.

Most of them were skilled weavers or other textile workers. New machines, such as shearing-frames or power looms, did the same work as they did but faster and cheaper (see page 10). They feared that their wages would be driven down and they would have to become unskilled factory hands. At the same time, the price of bread was very high. The Luddites sent threatening letters to employers with machines (Source 6). If the machines were not removed, gangs of workers would smash them with sledgehammers (see Source 7).

'Great Enoch still shall lead the van,
Stop him who dare, stop him who can'
went one of their songs.

> Sir,
> Information has just been given that you are a holder of those detestable shearing-frames and I was asked by my men to write to you to give you fair warning to pull them down. If they are not taken down by the end of the week I shall send at least 300 men to destroy them.
>
> Signed, NED LUDD

SOURCE 6
Luddite letter to the owner of shearing-frames.

SOURCE 7
'Great Enoch': large sledgehammer used by Luddites, made by Enoch Taylor of Marsden, West Yorkshire.

> 'They broke only the frames of such as have reduced men's wages. In one house last night they broke four frames out of six. The other two, which belonged to masters who had not lowered wages, they did not touch.'

SOURCE 8
Report from the *Leeds Mercury* newspaper, 1812.

Were the Luddites just a mob?

One newspaper of the time described how the Luddites marched in disciplined silence to the factory. They smashed the machines and were then called to order by their leader before marching off again. Source 8 also helps to answer this question.

'Captain Swing'

We have seen (see page 59) that farmworkers suffered from low wages and were often laid off in the winter. One of the few winter jobs which provided them with some paid work was THRESHING. In the 1820s many farmers were buying threshing machines. These could do several days' threshing in a few hours. In 1830 the price of bread rose and desperation faced many farmworkers.

Again the protesters used a made-up name to protect themselves: 'Captain Swing'. Source 9 shows a threatening letter sent to a farmer, demanding higher wages. All over southern England there were outbreaks of RICK burning in the summer of 1830 (see Source 10).

The reaction of the government to this kind of violent protest was harsh. Seventeen Luddites were hanged at York in 1812. Following the 'Captain Swing' riots, 19 were executed, 505 transported to Australia and 644 imprisoned.

ACTIVITY

1 Get into groups of four.
It is 1821 and you are all skilled hand-weavers. The price of bread has doubled in the last month and you all have families. A local factory-owner has bought a power loom and is turning out cloth at a much lower price than you can. Think about what you can and what you cannot do.
Think about the punishment if you break the law.
Think about your starving children.
What are you going to do about the situation?
Report to the class what you decide. If you decide to send any letters like Source 9, work out what to say.

2 Discuss this problem:
It is the present. You all work in an office writing out orders for goods as they come in from customers and sending them to the factory. The boss has plans to introduce a computerised system which will do the job in half the time. Only two of you will be needed.
What do you decide to say to the boss?

> this is to inform you
> what you have to undergo
> Gentelmen if providing you
> Dont pull down your nes:
> shenes and rise the poor
> mens wages the maried
> men give tow and six
> pence a day a day the
> singel tow shilings. or we
> will burn down your
> barns and you in them
> this is the last notis
> from W.B.R

SOURCE 9
Letter sent by 'Captain Swing' to a farmer, autumn 1830.

SOURCE 10
Hayricks set on fire by rioters.

What happened at Peterloo?

There was serious distress among working people in the years after the Napoleonic wars ended in 1815. The wartime demand for iron and textiles ceased, so workers were laid off. Thousands of ex-soldiers and sailors were looking for jobs. Food prices were high.

There were angry demonstrations in 1816 in London and protest marches in 1817. Ideas of DEMOCRACY and REFORM from the French Revolution were still alive. Some working people talked of revolution and began to train with weapons. On 16 August 1819 there was to be a big demonstration in St Peter's Fields, Manchester, to be addressed by the great reform speaker Henry Hunt.

Many middle-class people found this situation frightening. They thought working people should accept their position and not complain; they were opposed to any idea of change. They were suspicious of the demonstration and afraid of a revolution.

The local MAGISTRATES who were responsible for law and order called out the local YEOMANRY. These men were mostly opposed to the demonstrators. Soon the yeomanry got out of hand and charged into the crowd, armed with swords. Thirteen people were killed and many wounded. The event became known as 'Peterloo', a sarcastic reference to the victory over the French at the battle of Waterloo, four years earlier. Sources 11 to 16 present various impressions and accounts of these events.

'Before 12 o'clock crowds began to assemble, each village having a banner and some a cap with "Liberty" painted on it. Each party kept in military order, with sticks on their shoulders.'

[French revolutionaries wore 'caps of Liberty'.]

SOURCE 11
Extract from a report in *The Courier* newspaper.

I saw the march proceeding towards St Peter's Fields and never saw a happier sight. The so-called 'marching order' was what we often see in processions of Sunday School children. Our company laughed at the fears of the magistrates, and the remark was made that if the men intended mischief they would not have brought their wives and children with them.

SOURCE 12
Eye-witness account, from one of the demonstrators at Peterloo.

SOURCE 13
Part of a cartoon of events at St Peter's Fields, Manchester, on 16 August 1819.

'The event would have taken place without bloodshed if the mob had not attacked the soldiers with missiles. As a result, the cavalry charged in their own defence.'

SOURCE 14
Another extract from *The Courier*.

'They came in a threatening manner – they came with the banners of death, thereby showing they meant to overthrow the government. I believe you are a downright blackguard reformer. Some of you reformers ought to be hanged.'

SOURCE 15
Magistrate talking to one of the demonstrators.

A club of female reformers, 156 in number, from Oldham, had a white silk banner, inscribed 'Votes for All'.
The cavalry drew their swords and brandished them fiercely. Nothing was thrown at them. Not a pistol was fired during this period.

SOURCE 16
From an article in *The Times* newspaper.

SOURCE 17
Manchester in the 19th century.

attainment target 3

1 Using only the accounts from *The Courier* (Sources 11 and 14), who do you think was to blame for what happened at Peterloo?

2 Using only Sources 14 and 16, who do you think was to blame?

3 How useful is Source 12 for finding out about the demonstration?

4 Choose the two sources which you think are the most useful and the least useful for finding out about what happened. Explain your choices.

5 The cartoon, Source 13, was drawn afterwards. Whose side do you think the cartoonist was on? Does this mean that this source is unreliable?

6 Does Source 15 provide reliable evidence about: the demonstration? The attitude of the magistrates to the reformers?

7 How accurate an account can you make of events at Peterloo, using these sources?

How did Parliament change?

Look again at the picture of Sheffield on page 54 and compare it with Source 18. Before 1832 the great city of Sheffield, along with places like Birmingham, Manchester and Leeds had no MPs at all. Dunwich, Old Sarum and Bramber, on the other hand, had two MPs each.

These 'rotten boroughs', as they were called, were not the only aspect of the old Parliamentary system to be criticised. There were also 'pocket boroughs' where the voters did exactly what their landlord told them; they were 'in his pocket'. Most MPs were landowners from the south of England. In the past, this had reflected where the money and power lay. Now the industrial north and Midlands were becoming increasingly important. Industrialists did not think it was right that Parliament should be dominated by landowners. They objected to laws like the Corn Laws of 1815, which kept up the price of corn to help farmers.

The pressure for reform of Parliament continued after Peterloo. RADICALS like William Cobbett, Thomas Attwood and Francis Place wanted all adult males to have the vote. Many working people joined in the campaign. Huge meetings were held (see Source 19).

The Mirror
OF
LITERATURE, AMUSEMENT, AND INSTRUCTION.

No. 492.] SATURDAY, JUNE 4, 1831. [PRICE 2d.

THREE BOROUGHS

1.

2.

3.

Proposed to be wholly disfranchised by the REFORM BILL.
1. DUNWICH. 2. OLD SARUM. 3. BRAMBER.

VOL. XVII. 2 B

SOURCE 18
Three 'rotten boroughs', shown on the cover of a newspaper in 1831.

SOURCE 19
Reform meeting in Birmingham, 1832.

The WHIG PARTY could see that the system had to be changed but were afraid to give the vote to everyone. They thought that the working class were too undisciplined and too uneducated to be allowed to vote. They proposed that any male in a house worth £10 a year or more should have the right to vote. This would include middle-class male voters in the new industrial towns, but would exclude the working classes. The letter to the Whig leader, Lord Russell (Source 20), makes clear what the results of his proposals would be.

Many people were against changing the system (see Source 21). When the House of Lords rejected the Whig proposals there were riots in Bristol, Nottingham and Derby. Eventually the Reform Act was passed, in 1832.

The number of voters went up a little, to 700,000, about 8 per cent of the male population. The Act also gave 40 new towns and cities the right to elect their own MPs (see Source 22). Many working-class people were bitterly disappointed by the Act. It gave them nothing and was a main cause of the great Chartist movement, see pages 74–75.

Thirty-five years later, in 1867, the Conservative leader Disraeli gave the right to vote to working men in towns. Voting in secret was introduced in 1872. Only in 1884 was the right to vote extended to working men in rural areas. Women did not have equal voting rights with men until well into the 20th century.

'In the parts occupied by the working classes, not one householder in 50 would have a vote. In the streets occupied by shops, almost every householder would have a vote. In the town of Holbeck, containing 11,000 inhabitants, chiefly of the working classes, but with several respectable dwellings, there would be only 150 voters.'

SOURCE 20
Letter from Edward Baines, newspaper editor in Leeds, to Lord Russell, 1831. Baines explains how people in Leeds would be affected by giving the vote to those living in houses worth £10 or more per year.

'The present system has proved itself to be the best which ever had stood the test of experience and the nation was enjoying under it the highest degree of glory, prosperity, wealth and liberty.'

SOURCE 21
Opposition to reform, 1832.

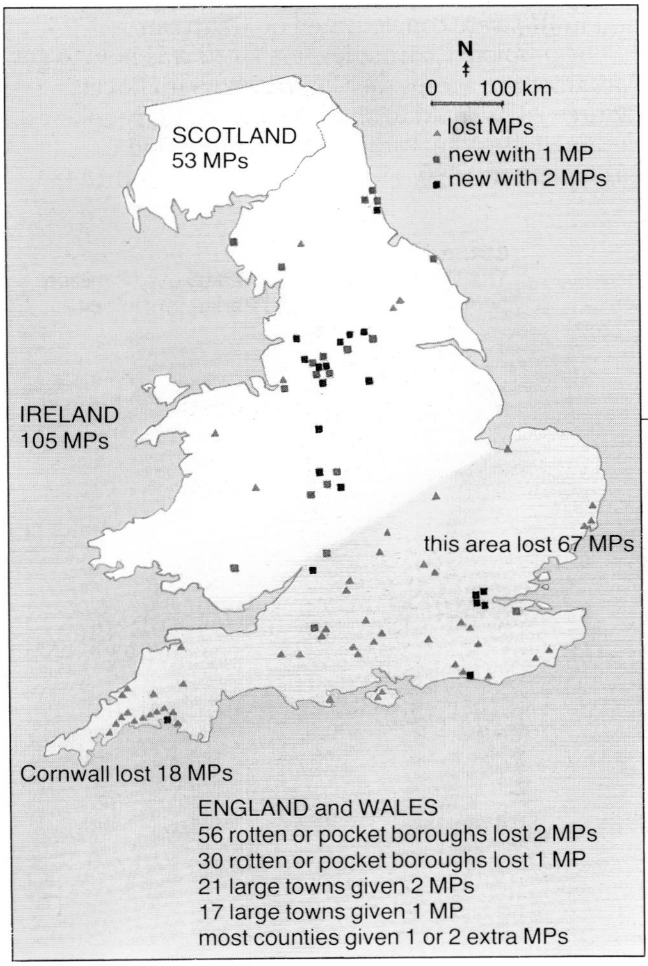

N
0 100 km
lost MPs
new with 1 MP
new with 2 MPs
SCOTLAND
53 MPs
IRELAND
105 MPs
this area lost 67 MPs
Cornwall lost 18 MPs
ENGLAND and WALES
56 rotten or pocket boroughs lost 2 MPs
30 rotten or pocket boroughs lost 1 MP
21 large towns given 2 MPs
17 large towns given 1 MP
most counties given 1 or 2 extra MPs

SOURCE 22
Map showing the changes brought about by the 1832 Reform Act.

1. How would someone who had been present at Peterloo react to the feelings in Source 21?
2. Why did the Whigs want to exclude working-class voters?
3. Why were women excluded from the vote for the whole of this period?
4. Why were working-class people disappointed with the 1832 Reform Act?
5. Do you think the 1832 Reform Act was a great change or a great disappointment?

What did Chartists want?

Working-class reformers said they had been 'bitterly and basely deceived' by the 1832 Reform Act. Their mass demonstrations had helped to get the Act passed, but they gained nothing from it. Some of the actions of the new Parliament, such as passing the Poor Law Amendment Act, 1834 (see page 86), made life worse for working people. The trial of the Tolpuddle Martyrs (see page 80) led many to lose hope in trade union activity. The further reform of Parliament seemed the best hope for the future. Working-class MPs could then pass laws to solve working people's problems.

A charter was published in 1838, with six basic points:

- A vote for all adult males
- Secret ballots (so that employers could not influence how a worker voted)
- Annual parliaments (to keep MPs in touch with voters)
- No property qualification for MPs (so that working people could stand)
- Payment of MPs (also to allow working people to stand)
- Equal sized constituencies.

Chartism was the first really working-class movement. There were Chartist groups in most towns and cities. They sent delegates to national conventions, entirely organised and paid for by working people's efforts and money. Working-class women took part too and had their own organisations.

'The Charter means meat and drink and clothing, good hours and good beds, and good furniture for every man and woman and child who will do a fair day's work.'

SOURCE 23
From a speech by the Chartist Bronterre O'Brien.

'Let us, Friends, unite together the honest, moral, hard-working and thinking members of society. Let us obtain a library of books. Let us publish our views so that we create a moral, thinking, energetic force in politics.'

SOURCE 24
From a speech by Chartist leader William Lovett, 1838.

The 1840s were difficult times for working people, with factories closing and high food prices. As Source 23 explains, the hopes of millions of people for a decent life were concentrated on Chartism.

The problem Chartist leaders faced was how to get Parliament to accept the Charter. William Lovett (Source 24) wanted to show that working people deserved the vote. Petitions were presented to Parliament in 1839, 1842 (see Source 25) and 1848.

SOURCE 25
The Chartist petition, signed by over 3 million people, being carried to Parliament in 1842.

What if Parliament rejected it?

Many Chartists were so desperate, so angry and so shut out of power that they thought about an armed rebellion (see Source 26). After the 1839 petition was rejected there was a rebellion in Newport, South Wales. Twenty Chartists, mostly miners, were killed (see Source 27). After the 1842 petition was rejected, there were calls for an armed rising and there was a general strike in Lancashire. When the 1848 petition was rejected, Chartism went into decline.

The confusion between peaceful or forceful tactics counted against the Chartists. If they were peaceful, why did some threaten violence? If they were violent the government was ready, with a large army under General Napier. Even armed Chartists knew they did not stand a chance.

Chartism seemed to have failed. However, the movement had inspired many working-class people. They went into other activities: trade unions, cooperatives, newspapers, temperance leagues. Eventually, five of the six demands of the Charter were met.

'A great many people were arming themselves with guns or picks. I bought a gun, although I knew it was a serious thing for a Chartist to have a gun in his possession. It might be said that we were fools, but young people now have no idea what we had to endure. From 1842 to 1848 I did not average 9 shillings (45p) a week.'

SOURCE 26
Benjamin Wilson, an old Chartist, writing in 1887.

attainment target 1

1. Why did so many people support Chartism?
2. What different attitudes to Chartism are described in Sources 23 and 24?
3. Why did Benjamin Wilson, Source 26, buy a gun?
4. What different attitudes to Chartism might the following people have: a navvy; the wife of a Northumberland miner; a Suffolk landowner and MP; a middle-class woman shopkeeper in Manchester; an engine driver?

SOURCE 27
Chartists attacking the hotel at Newport, South Wales, where their leader was under arrest, 1839.

People on the move

People were on the move in the 19th century in a way they never had been before. We have seen (page 51) how people were moving to the cities from the country. Even as late as 1900, two thirds of London policemen and transport workers had been born in the country. But people were moving further than that, both into and out of Britain.

Emigration

Source 28 shows the huge numbers of people who emigrated from Britain. Part of the reason for increasing emigration was that better railways and steamships made travel easier. The main reasons, however, were strong 'push' reasons persuading them to leave, and strong 'pull' reasons attracting them.

The 'push' reasons are clear from this book: the hard living, the low wages, the failure of Chartism and early trade unions. It was disgust with Britain which led people to leave their homes and travel halfway across the world to an unknown land. Even so, their feelings on leaving may have been mixed, as the artist of Source 29 suggests.

The 'pull' reasons were the attractions of new lands in America, Canada, Australia and elsewhere. Advertisements, like Source 30, were put in newspapers. Cheap farming land, steady jobs, good wages and better housing were the hopes of the emigrants. Many hoped, too, that their new countries would be more democratic than Britain (see Source 31). The gold rushes, to California in 1849, and later to Australia and then South Africa, attracted hundreds of people.

	1861–1870	1881–1890	Total 1851–1920
USA	442,000	1,008,000	4,651,000
Canada	90,000	257,000	2,856,000
Australia	184,000	317,000	2,102,000
Others	37,000	162,000	1,606,000
Total	753,000	1,124,000	11,215,000

SOURCE 28
Numbers and destinations of people emigrating from Britain.

SOURCE 29
'The Last of England', painting by Ford Maddox Brown (1821–1893).

Free emigration to South Australia
via Southampton

We are authorised by Her Majesty's Colonial Land and Emigration Commissioners to grant a free passage, by first-class ship, to the healthy and prosperous colony of South Australia to agricultural labourers, shepherds, male and female servants, miners of good character. The demand for labour in the colony is urgent, with good pay ensuring the comfort of every well-conducted man and his family.

SOURCE 30
Advertisement in the *Northampton Herald*, 1839.

Dear Mother and Father,
I like the country here very much, but my wife does not seem so well contented yet. I got work the first day that I was here and have had plenty of work ever since. Farmers and labourers all sit at one table here. I don't wish to persuade anyone to come over for they must expect to see a good many hardships. But I know that a poor man can do a great deal better here than at home.

SOURCE 31
Letter from Canada by George Sullington.

Official help

Several different groups also encouraged emigration. Population was rising in rural areas, and so was the cost of looking after the rural poor. Some landlords paid the fares of farmworkers for this reason. In Petworth, Sussex, in 1834 Lord Egremont helped charter the ship *British Tar* to take 200 emigrants to Canada.

Trade unions helped emigration because they thought that too many people looking for work kept everyone's wages down. Queen Victoria's husband, Prince Albert, helped people wanting to emigrate from the Scottish Highlands. The government wanted British people living in their colonies; hence the free passage offered in Source 30.

Most early emigrants were single men. The government wanted settlers to remain in their colonies, so encouraged young women to emigrate. In 1833 young women 'of good health and character' could emigrate to Australia for £6.

At such prices, conditions on board ship had to be basic. Up to 700 passengers might be crowded on board for the 35-day trip across the Atlantic (see Source 32).

1 What attractions does the advertisement in Source 30 offer?

2 What does George Sullington like about Canada (Source 31)?

3 What do you think the people in Source 29 are thinking?

4 What does Source 29 tell us about emigrants, and about the artist's view of emigrants?

5 RACISM uses stereotypes: it gives general labels to all members of a particular group, instead of looking at them as individuals. What stereotypes does the author of Source 33 use?

6 What emotional language does he also use?

SOURCE 32
Emigrants on board ship.

Immigration

The Irish famine of 1842 led millions of Irish people to emigrate, some to the USA, many to England and Scotland. The lowest paid jobs and the worst housing was often all that they were offered. They also met hostility from local people. Racist attitudes appeared (see Source 33). From the 1880s Jews began to flee to Britain, escaping persecution in Russia. Jewish communities were established in London and some northern cities, and received some racist hostility.

'The rapid growth of the cotton industry has attracted workers here from every part of the kingdom and Ireland has poured forth the most destitute of their hordes to supply the increasing demand for labour. This IMMIGRATION has been a serious evil . . . Want of cleanliness, of forethought and carefulness are found in alliance with drunkenness, reckless habits and disease.'

SOURCE 33
Written by J. P. Kay Shuttleworth in 1832.

Religious differences

For poor people facing hardships of all kinds, religion was often the only thing that made life bearable. Many people went to church or CHAPEL twice or three times on Sundays. In addition, many leisure activities were centred around the church: there were church teas, choirs, outings, Bible studies, parades and bands. Sunday Schools provided the only education many children had. Many middle-class families held daily prayers (Source 34).

A religious census was held in 1851. It showed that 7 million people were actively involved in religion out of a total population of 18 million. Of these 52 per cent were at Church of England (Anglican) churches, 21 per cent at Methodist chapels, 20 per cent at other Nonconformist chapels and 4 per cent at Roman Catholic churches.

In many British towns and cities, and in rural Wales, much less than half the people who went to church attended Anglican churches.

The Church of England was obviously losing its grip on the nation. It was still powerful: all posts in the Army, the Navy, the Civil Service and the law were reserved for Anglicans. The monarch was (and is) Head of the Church and bishops had seats in the House of Lords.

The strength of the Church of England was in the villages, where the parson and the squire ruled together. Class differences were made clear in the parish church. The better-off could rent a more comfortable pew, and took communion before the poorer villagers (see Source 28, page 59). The parson preached a message of obedience: God had made the rich to own land and give orders, the poor to work hard and obey (see Source 35).

The rapid growth of towns and cities was largely ignored by the Church of England. People moving away from the villages were only too ready to leave the church behind as well.

SOURCE 34
Painting of a 19th century family and servants at daily prayers.

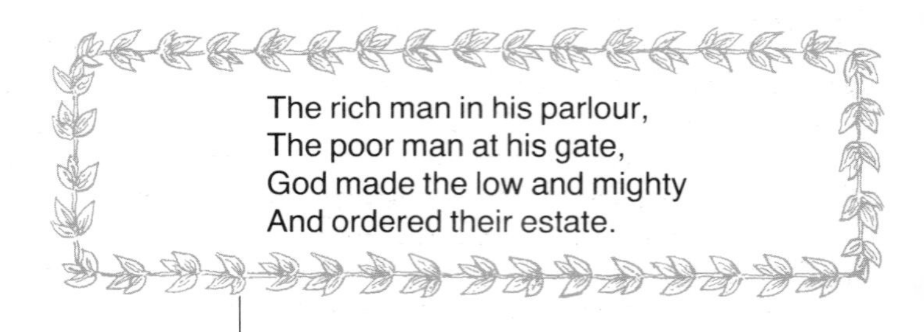

The rich man in his parlour,
The poor man at his gate,
God made the low and mighty
And ordered their estate.

SOURCE 35
Verse from 19th century Anglican hymn.

The Methodists

Into this gap came the Methodists. Their founder, John Wesley, was trained as an Anglican. When he was a student he worked out a methodical series of prayers and study. This earned him the label 'Methodist'. In 1738 he had a deep religious experience. He began to preach to anyone who would listen and made a special effort to visit those people and places the other churches ignored. Source 36 describes a big open-air meeting he held in Cornwall. He travelled 200,000 miles and preached 40,000 sermons in the last 53 years of his life. His message was simple: stop drinking, gambling, swearing and lead a sober, Christian life or you will go to Hell.

'It was estimated that there were 10,000 people. I could not stop until it was so dark that we could scarce see one another; and there was on all sides the deepest attention; none speaking, stirring or looking aside.'

SOURCE 36
From John Wesley's journal, 1873.

> Dare to be a Daniel,
> Dare to stand alone,
> Dare to have a purpose true,
> Dare to make it known.

SOURCE 37
Verse from a Methodist hymn.

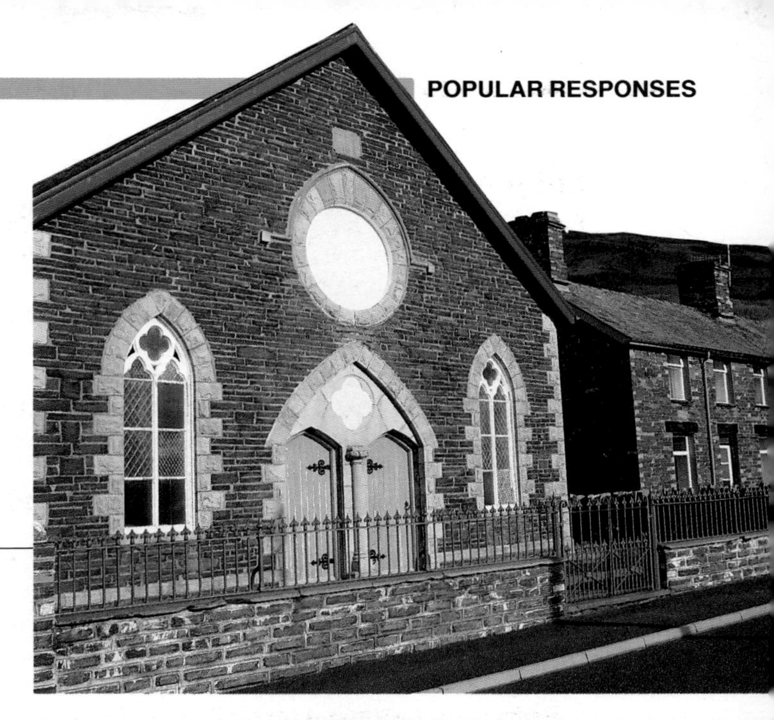

SOURCE 38
Nineteenth century Welsh chapel.

Wesley did not want to set up his own church but in 1784 he split from the Church of England. The organisation he devised for the Methodist Church was very effective. Twelve people joined together and formed a 'class'. They met in each other's houses and held their own services. A group of classes could join up to build a chapel and perhaps appoint a MINISTER.

Methodism had a tremendous impact on ordinary people all over Britain. They reacted to the stirring hymns and powerful sermons. But they also learnt to take control of their own lives. They became confident that they were as good as the next person in the sight of God (see Source 37). They learnt to speak in public, and to run their own affairs. It is no wonder that so many early trade unionists were Methodists (see page 80).

Other Nonconformists, such as the Baptists and Congregationalists, also had a wide appeal. This was especially true in Wales. The Church of England was weak and out of touch in industrial areas, and in Wales it never had been strong. The Nonconformists seemed closer to people's lives; their ministers often preached in Welsh. New chapels were built, the focus of many Welsh communities (Source 38).

For some groups, like the Quakers, religion meant trying to help other people. Elizabeth Fry spent her life working among prisoners in dreadful prison conditions. The Cadbury family built the village of Bournville to house the workers in their chocolate factory (Source 39).

Evangelicals

Some members of the Church of England, called Evangelicals, felt the same way. They worked for the abolition of slavery and child labour as well as reform of working conditions in factories and mines (see page 84).

SOURCE 39
Children in the garden of a house in Bournville, the village built by the Quaker Cadbury family.

attainment target 1

1 Give one difference between the place of religion in people's lives today compared with the 19th century.

2 How does the importance of religion in 19th century Britain compare with the situation in any other period you have studied?

3 Choose three examples from these pages which show different aspects of religion in 19th century Britain.

4 Explain the part religion played in each of the aspects you have chosen.

How much could working people help themselves?

Some working people did not hope for political change. Instead they worked at improving their working lives. Wage cuts, dangerous work, long hours and sudden lay-offs all threatened their livelihood (look back at pages 22–23). As individuals they were completely at the mercy of their employers and could simply be sacked if they complained. But if all workers combined together, their employer would have to listen to them or lose the entire workforce.

Early trade unions

A trade union is an organisation for all workers in a particular trade. Some kinds of trade union had existed for centuries, but in the panic over French revolutionary ideas coming to Britain (see page 67) the government banned them in 1799 and 1800. In 1824 unions were made legal again. Source 40 shows a membership card from one of the first unions for women workers.

In 1834 Robert Owen founded a union for all workers, called the Grand National Consolidated Trade Union (GNCTU). In the village of Tolpuddle, Dorset, George Loveless, his brother James and four other farm labourers formed a branch of the GNCTU. They were fighting a reduction in wages from 9 shillings (45p) a week to 8 shillings (40p).

UNITED TO PROTECT

The Bearer

Ellen Riely

Has been admitted a Member of the WEST OF SCOTLAND Power Loom Female Weavers Society

Glasgow 22 March 1833 No. 5701

SOURCE 40
Membership card of the Union of Power Loom Female Weavers, 1833.

The government was worried by the GNCTU as it seemed to interfere with their ideas of 'laissez-faire' (see page 62). Local JPs in Dorset had the six Tolpuddle labourers arrested. The government suggested they could be charged with taking an illegal oath, under a law of 1797. George Loveless, a Methodist lay preacher, gave a dignified speech at his trial. Although they had only committed a minor offence, they were sentenced to transportation to Australia for 7 years. They were pardoned in 1836, but it was 1839 before the last of the six returned. The GNCTU collapsed and many workers turned to Chartism.

SOURCE 41
Modern reconstruction of the inside of the Cooperative shop, Rochdale, Lancashire, opened in 1844. This became the model for other Cooperative Societies.

Cooperatives

In 1844 seven weavers in Rochdale, Lancashire, got together with 21 others and each put in £1. With this they bought butter, sugar, flour, oatmeal and candles, and set up a little shop (Source 41). They opened the shop in the evenings and sold goods, at fair prices, to local people. Their profits were distributed among the customers. Money was also put aside for a school in the room above the shop, and a library.

Out of this effort to help each other in practical ways by their efforts grew the huge Cooperative movement, with shops and factories all over Britain.

New Model Unions

In the 1850s and 1860s unions of skilled workers began to grow (see Source 42). Engineers, carpenters and bricklayers, for example, were well paid, earning up to £1.75 a week. They could afford to pay a high SUBSCRIPTION, say 1 shilling (5p) a week. This paid for a full-time Secretary and a good organisation. They paid all kinds of benefits to their members (see Source 43) and avoided strikes. They seemed a 'model' for others to follow. These 'New Model Unions' joined together to start the Trades Union Congress (TUC) in 1868.

At the same time, hostility between workers and employers sometimes led to violence. If workers went on strike, an employer could hire others to do their jobs. These strike-breakers were called 'blacklegs'. Sometimes blacklegs were threatened (see Source 44), and violence occurred.

The government decided to investigate trade unions and set up an enquiry. They were impressed with people like Robert Applegarth of the Carpenters' Union and William Allen of the Engineers'. They decided it would be better to make unions legal and this was done by the Trade Union Act of 1871. From then on union membership began to increase.

SOURCE 42
Emblem of the Operative Bricklayers' Society.

> 'The aims of this society are to raise funds to help members in cases of sickness, accident or old age, for the burial of members and their wives, emigration, loss of tools by fire, water or theft and for assistance to members who are out of work.'

SOURCE 43
Robert Applegarth, Secretary to the Carpenters' Union, giving evidence to the Parliamentary Commission on Trade Unions, 1867.

> On Saturday last I met the prisoner in Wardour Street, when she said to me 'Well, Mrs Mills, you are doing the dirty work, are you?' I asked her what she meant, and she said 'You are fetching work from the shops that are on strike.' I asked her if that had anything to do with her and she replied 'Yes, it's all to do with me. It's stinking hussies such as you who are keeping the men out of work, you stinking cow. When this strike is over I will do for you.'

SOURCE 44
Mrs Mills speaking about Ellen Meade, who was convicted of attacking a non-union worker during a strike.

1. What evidence is there on these pages of the law being used against trade unionists?
2. Why was Ellen Meade angry with Mrs Mills (see Source 44)?
3. Do you think Ellen Meade's actions, as described by Mrs Mills, were wrong?
4. Why do you think the government were impressed by trade unionists like Robert Applegarth (Source 43)?
5. Why would it be difficult for most workers to set up a New Model Union?
6. Trade unions are still controversial. Is any member of your family a trade union member? Which union? What does the union do for them? Is any member of your family hostile to trade unions? What do they dislike about them?
7. Do you think the story on these pages is one of success or failure for working people?

The voice of the working class

The workers in the New Model Unions were the aristocrats of employees. Industry could not work without their skills and they used this to get what they wanted without having to go on strike. But what about those at the bottom of the heap, the unskilled labourers?

These included the matchgirls who made matches at Bryant and May's factory in the east end of London (see Source 45). Apart from the conditions described in Source 46, they also got a disease called 'phossy jaw' from the phosphorus in the matches. Annie Besant helped organise a strike of the matchgirls and won support for them through her newspaper articles. Within three weeks they had won better wages and conditions.

Then there were the gas-workers, who spent long hours shovelling coal. Will Thorne formed a gas-workers' union in 1889, and won a reduction in hours.

Another large group of unskilled workers were the London dockers, paid by the hour to unload ships. Their harsh treatment and lack of security is described in Source 47. In 1889 they went on strike for a wage of 6d (2½p) an hour, known as the 'dockers' tanner'. They had good leaders, like Ben Tillett and John Burns (Source 48). They managed to hold out for several weeks, helped by money from other unions and from the Australian dockers' union. Ships could not unload at the docks; their cargoes rotted in their holds. The employers gave in and paid them 6d an hour.

SOURCE 45
Annie Besant (sixth from right) and members of the matchgirls' strike committee, 1888.

> Born in slums, driven to work while still children, under-sized because under-fed, oppressed because helpless, flung aside as soon as worked out.
>
> The starting time is 6.30 in summer and 8.00 in winter. Work finishes at 6 p.m. The girls have to stand the whole time. A typical girl earns 4 shillings (20p) a week.

SOURCE 46
From a newspaper article by Annie Besant, called 'White Slavery in London', 1888.

> 'We were driven into a shed, iron-barred from end to end. Outside the foremen walked up and down, like dealers in a cattle market, picking and choosing from a crowd of men who, in their eagerness for work, trampled each other underfoot.'

SOURCE 47
Description of workers on the London Docks by Ben Tillett.

SOURCE 48
John Burns addressing dockers at a strike meeting in 1889.

SOURCE 49
Mineworkers' Union banner showing Keir Hardie.

These 'new unions' of unskilled workers could only collect a small subscription, 1d or 2d a week. They paid only one benefit: strike pay. Their leaders were more aggressive at using strikes to win better pay for their members. Ben Tillett simply said, 'It is the work of the trade unionist to stamp out poverty.'

This is not a simple success story for unions, however. Times were hard in the 1890s. Employers fought back, combining together and using 'blackleg' labour. Will Thorne's gasworkers lost a strike in 1890. The Dockers' Union collapsed in 1891. Even the engineers lost a big strike in 1897–1898. Once again workers turned to Parliament to try to improve their position.

The Labour Party

Annie Besant, Ben Tillett, Will Thorne and John Burns were socialists. That is, they opposed the capitalist system in which trade and industry are controlled by private owners for their own profit. Socialists followed the ideas of Karl Marx, that workers and employers were bound to be in conflict. They believed that industry and banks should be run by the government, for the benefit of all.

After 1884 all men had the vote, but there was no working-class party to belong to. The two political parties were Liberals and Conservatives. Sometimes working-class MPs were elected, but sat with the Liberals. In 1892 James Keir Hardie (see Source 49) was elected MP for West Ham, and in the following year he set up the Independent Labour Party, a working-class party. Socialists from around the country supported him, but their numbers were few and they had little money.

The key to mass support and funds had to come from the trade union movement. In 1899 the TUC set up the Labour Representation Committee (LRC) to get more working-class, socialist MPs elected to Parliament. In the 1906 Election 29 LRC MPs were elected, and called themselves the Labour Party.

1. What part did each of the following play in the matchgirls' strike and the dockers' strike?
   Good leaders Popular support
   Support of other unions Socialism
   Workers sticking together (solidarity)
2. Why did the strikes of the 1890s fail?
3. Explain how socialist ideas and trade union backing combined to form the Labour Party.

What could Parliament do for working people?

Evangelicals (see page 79) felt moved by their religion to help the poor and needy. Along with practical help, the needy had a strong dose of religion (see Source 50). Evangelicals also played a large part in passing Acts of Parliament to improve working conditions in factories and mines.

By 1830 there were 2,500 factories in the textile industry. As we have seen, they employed men, women and children in stuffy and dangerous conditions, for very long hours. Union leaders, such as John Doherty of the Lancashire Cotton Spinners, campaigned for a '10-hour day' for all.

It was not going to be easy to get Parliament to pass a law to restrict their working day to 10 hours. Only middle-class people had the vote and many of them knew nothing about factories. Factory-owners had friends in Parliament. They were afraid of losing their profits if hours were cut. Believers in 'laissez-faire' felt it was wrong to pass laws to interfere between employers and employees (see Source 51). The 10 Hours' Movement worked with Evangelical supporters such as Richard Oastler, Michael Sadler and Lord Shaftesbury. They felt they could win over public opinion by emphasising the effect of long hours on children. If children's hours were cut then adult workers would benefit too.

In 1831 Richard Oastler wrote a powerful letter to a newspaper (Source 52). Michael Sadler asked Parliament to restrict hours of work to 10. Parliament set up a committee to investigate and hear witnesses (see Sources 53 and 54). This evidence was published and the British public were shocked.

> Let the truth speak out. Thousands of our fellow creatures, both female and male, the inhabitants of a Yorkshire town are at this moment existing in a state of slavery, compelled by the dread of the strap of the overlooker to hasten half-dressed, but not half-fed, to the worsted mills of Bradford. Thousands of little children, from 7 to 14 years, are daily compelled to labour from six in the morning to seven in the evening – Britons blush while you read this.

SOURCE 52
From an article by Richard Oastler in the *Leeds Mercury*, 1830.

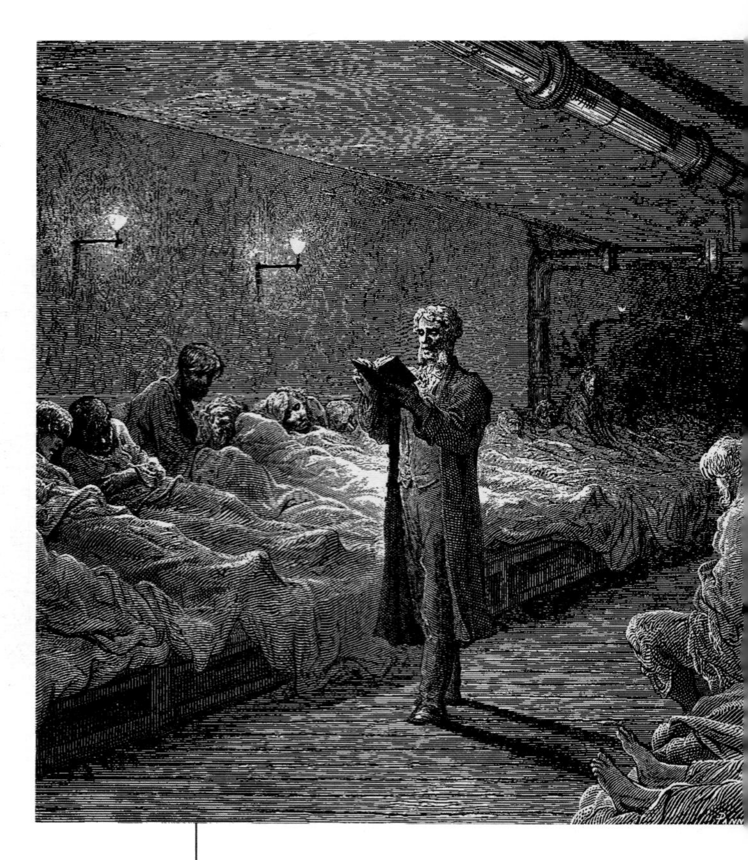

SOURCE 50
Bible reading at a church hostel for the homeless in London.

> 'Have those who are in favour of this [the 10 Hours' Movement] thought that it would be the first example of the laws of a free country interfering with the freedom of adult labour? Have they considered that if spinners and weavers are protected by Act of Parliament then a thousand others must, in justice, have their claims attended to?'

SOURCE 51
Letter from Richard Cobden, 1836.

> 'I really do think it is necessary that children should be protected from excessive labour. That is the first point, and with the hope, I confess, that it will benefit myself and others as well.'

SOURCE 53
Evidence of David Brook, clothworker, to Sadler's Committee, 1831.

Questioner: Were you originally a straight and healthy boy?
Joseph Hebergram: Yes, I was straight and healthy when I was 7. When I had worked about half a year a weakness fell in my knees and ankles. In the morning I could scarcely walk and my brother and sister used to take me under each arm and run with me to the mill. If we were five minutes late the overlooker would take a strap and beat us until we were black and blue.

SOURCE 54
Evidence to Sadler's Committee, 1831.

SOURCE 55
Picture from the 1842 Parliamentary Report on Conditions in the Mines.

Then an election was held. Sadler lost his seat and Lord Shaftesbury took over the leadership in Parliament. An Act was passed, but it only cut the hours of children: no child under 9 could work; 9–13 year olds to work no more than 8 hours, plus 2 hours of school. Middle-class opinion was pleased, but the 10 Hours' Movement was bitterly disappointed. Adults still had to work 12–16 hours. The 10-hour day was not achieved until 1853.

Mines Act, 1842

Lord Shaftesbury turned his attention to the terrible working conditions in coalmines. Another Commission was set up, evidence was heard and published, with illustrations (see Source 55). It emphasised the employment of children and women. No thought was given to safety and hours of work for men or how women would find a living if they did not work in the pit.

Nevertheless, as Shaftesbury said: 'The disgust is very great, thank God.' The 1842 Mines Act said that no female or any boy under 10 should work underground.

attainment target 3

1. Look at Source 52. This article was designed to horrify people. What aspects of factory conditions does Oastler concentrate on to do this?
2. Does the fact that the letter was meant to horrify people mean that it is unreliable evidence of factory conditions?
3. What does Source 53 tell us about the campaign to reduce hours of work?
4. What harmful effects of factory work are emphasised in Source 54?
5. Some witnesses had their stories rehearsed. Does this affect the reliability of Source 54?
6. What does Source 53 tell us about the real aims of the 10 Hours' Movement?
7. The artist who drew Source 55 had not been down a coalmine but drew the picture from what witnesses said. What use is this source to us?

Dealing with the poor

What should be done about people in need? Your answer to this question will depend on what you think are the reasons for poverty. If you think people are poor through their own fault, you will have one kind of answer; if you think it is not their own fault, you will have another solution. It is a controversial issue, now and in the period covered by this book.

The Old Poor Law

When you studied *The Making of the UK* you might have looked at how poor people were looked after in Tudor and Stuart times. Britain at that time was mainly rural, and each parish had to look after its own poor. People who were too old or too ill to work were given money ('outdoor relief') to help them live in their own homes. People who could work, the 'able-bodied poor', were given work and food in workhouses. This was the 'Old Poor Law', although every parish had slight differences.

The changes described in this book had put this system under great strain. In agricultural areas the population rise meant that too many people had too little work. The result was very low wages. In many areas this was made up to a living wage by giving money from the poor rate. In industrial areas the ups and downs of trade meant that sometimes hardly anyone needed help, and at other times hundreds did.

It was poverty which was behind people's protests, such as the 'Captain Swing' riots (see page 69) and the agitation for reform of Parliament in 1830–1832 (see pages 72–73). However, it was the middle classes who set about changing the system. Here are two very different interpretations of what happened:

SOURCE 59
London workhouse in 1809.

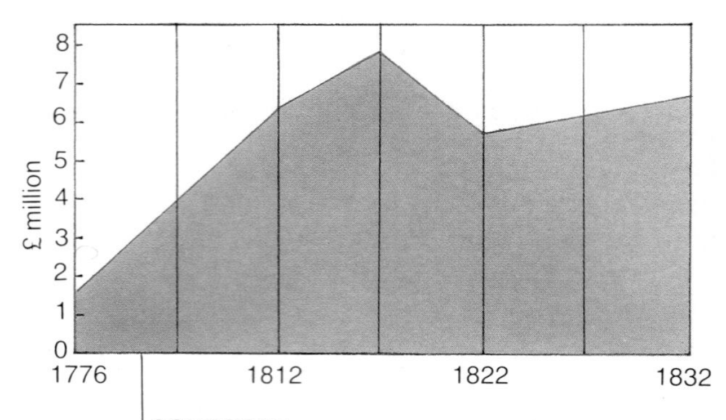

SOURCE 57
Costs of the poor rate in England and Wales, 1776–1832.

'The labouring poor always live hand to mouth. All they have above their needs of the moment goes to the alehouse. The poor laws of England lessen the will to save and weaken the incentive to soberness and hard work, and hence to happiness.'

SOURCE 58
The Reverend Thomas Malthus, 1797.

The New Poor Law: interpretation 1

The Old Poor Law was far too expensive (see Source 57). As Thomas Malthus said, it is no good giving the poor money as they only spend it on beer (Source 58). Outdoor relief made working people feel they need not bother to look for work as they got money anyhow. Workhouses were far too pleasant (see Source 59).

Those who believed this, like Edwin Chadwick (page 88), believed that people had to learn to stand on their own feet, and should not be looked after. The Poor Law Amendment Act in 1834 took up many of his ideas. Parishes were to be combined into unions, and workhouses built. Conditions in the workhouses were to be worse than those of poor people outside, so that people would make an effort to look after themselves. Men, women and children were to be separated, in different buildings (see Source 60), although parents could see their children every day (Source 61). The idea behind this separation was that poor parents would have no more children, and children would learn to work. Food was adequate (Source 62). Inmates wore uniform and were not allowed out. Old and ill people were also looked after separately.

The New Poor Law was successful because the cost of poor relief fell from £6.75 million before the Act to £4.5 million by 1839.

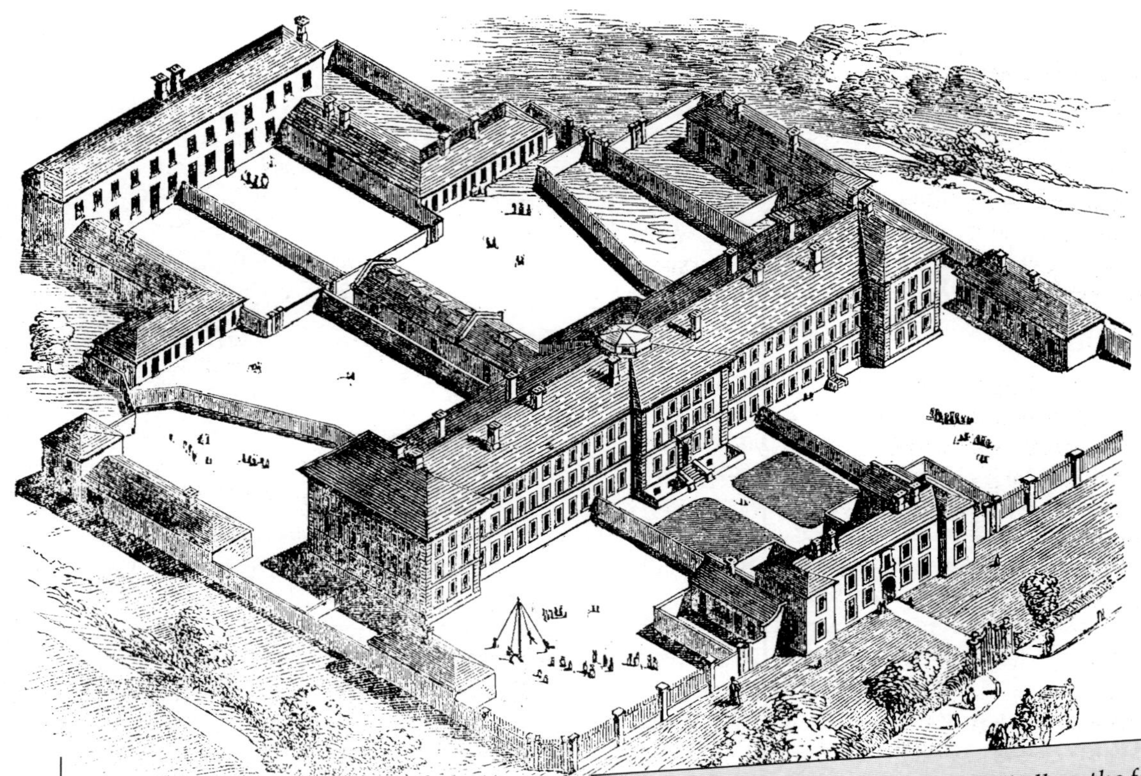

SOURCE 60
Fulham and Hammersmith Workhouse, built in 1849 for the New Poor Law.

'The Master of the workhouse shall allow the father or mother of any child in the workhouse to have an interview with such child at one time each day.'

SOURCE 61
One of the workhouse rules under the New Poor Law.

		BREAKFAST		DINNER				SUPPER		
		Bread	Gruel	Cooked Meat with Vegetables	Lobscouse	Soup with Vegetables	Suet Pudding	Bread	Cheese	Broth Thick'ned
		oz.	Pints	oz.	Pints	Pints	oz.	oz.	oz.	Pints
Sunday	Men	7	1½	6	–	–	–	5	–	1½
	Women	6	1½	5	–	–	–	4	–	1½
Monday	Men	7	1½	–	–	1½	–	6	2	–
	Women	6	1½	–	–	1½	–	5	2	–
Tuesday	Men	7	1½	–	–	–	14	6	2	–
	Women	6	1½	–	–	–	12	5	2	–
Wednesday	Men	7	1½	6	–	–	–	5	–	1½
	Women	6	1½	5	–	–	–	4	–	1½
Thursday	Men	7	1½	–	–	1½	–	6	2	–
	Women	6	1½	–	–	1½	–	5	2	–
Friday	Men	7	1½	–	2	–	–	6	2	–
	Women	6	1½	–	2	–	–	5	2	–
Saturday	Men	7	1½	–	–	–	14	6	2	–
	Women	6	1½	–	–	–	12	5	2	–

SOURCE 62
Food given in the workhouse under the New Poor Law.

The New Poor Law: interpretation 2

The Old Poor Law treated the poor like human beings. The cost of poor relief had fallen (see Source 57). Thomas Malthus (Source 58) and Edwin Chadwick (page 88) were comfortably off, middle-class men who did not understand how ordinary people could become poor. The old workhouses were basic but reasonable places because many people were there for reasons beyond their control (see Source 59).

The Poor Law Amendment Act of 1834 was cruel. It was terrible to separate families in large, frightening buildings (see Source 60). Rules like Source 61 treated people like prisoners. The food was boring (Source 62).

In industrial areas, bad trade might lead to a factory closing for a few months. It was no good putting hundreds of people in the workhouse: they would not be able to work when the factory re-opened again. There were anti-Poor Law riots in Huddersfield, Dewsbury, Todmorden, Stockport and elsewhere.

Opposition to the Act caused many to support Chartism (see pages 74–75) or to emigrate (see page 76). The Poor Law Amendment Act was one of the most hated acts of Parliament there has ever been.

attainment target 2

1. Compare these two accounts of the New Poor Law. How do they both use: the same facts, different facts, opinions and sources to tell quite different stories?

Public health and education

On page 62 we saw that governments in the early 19th century had a 'laissez-faire' attitude; that is, they did not want to interfere in people's lives. Two aspects of life in Britain which badly needed to be improved by law were public health and education. Yet it was not until the 1870s that really effective laws for each were passed.

Public health

The fast-growing towns and cities of industrial Britain were extremely unhealthy places (see page 55). As Sources 63 and 64 remind us, they were without drains, sewers, rubbish disposal and piped water supply. Yet those who wanted to change this situation were opposed every step of the way. The opponents objected to spending money and to being told what to do by the government in London.

One of those who wanted to improve public health was Edwin Chadwick. His work on poverty showed him that illness often caused people to become poor, because it stopped them working. Chadwick argued that if health was improved, poverty would be less.

He carried out an investigation into public health and published a 'Report on the Sanitary Condition of the Labouring Population' in 1842. He gave away 10,000 copies of the report and 20,000 were sold. The nation was shocked, but nothing was done.

> Imagine acre upon acre* of little streets without a paving-stone on the surface or a sewer beneath, deep trodden-churned sloughs of mud . . . Imagine such a surface drenched with the liquid slops which each family flings out daily . . . Indeed pigs are more common in some parts of Leeds than dogs and cats are in others.
>
> [*area of land; 1 acre = 0.4 hectares or 4047 square metres]

SOURCE 63
Description of Leeds in 1848.

It took a dreadful cholera epidemic in 1848, which killed 53,000 people, to bring change. Parliament passed the 1848 Public Health Act. Local Health Boards could be set up to take over all public health matters if the death rate was high or local people requested it.

Some towns and cities took this up and built sewers (see Source 36, page 62). But opposition continued (see Source 65) and nothing was done in many towns. Only after working men in towns got the vote, in 1867, did government act. The Public Health Act of 1875 made it compulsory to appoint sanitary inspectors and lay on sewers, drains and a water supply.

SOURCE 64
'Dirty Father Thames' – cartoon of 1848.

> 'We prefer to take our chance with cholera than to be bullied into health. There is nothing a man hates so much as being cleansed against his will, or having his floors swept, his hall whitewashed, his dung heaps cleared away. It is a fact that many people have died from a good washing.'

SOURCE 65
Extract from *The Times*, 1854.

Education

There were very few schools in late 18th century Britain. Upper-class children were taught by a tutor at home, or went to a public (boarding) school. Middle-class children would go to a grammar school. Working parents might send their younger children to a dame school and older ones to a common day school. Some of those were good, but some were really only child-minders. 'It is not much they pay me and it is not much I teach them,' as one dame said.

Some people thought education for all children was a bad thing (see Source 66). The Industrial Revolution brought a call for more education for two reasons: first, the need for more educated people to work machines and deal with paperwork; second, the need to keep young city children under control.

The second reason led Robert Raikes to set up the first Sunday School in 1780. He wanted to stop children playing about on their one day off, Sundays, and to teach them reading, writing, Christianity, obedience and good manners. In the 19th century churches and chapels set up many schools for weekdays too. They charged a small fee and were not compulsory.

The government started making a grant to education from 1833 and by the 1860s this had risen to £400,000 a year. It set up the Newcastle Commission to look into providing 'sound, cheap, elementary instruction to all classes of people'. One result of the search for cheapness was the system of 'payments by results'. Each school received a visit from an inspector once a year. The inspector would test the pupils and the teacher's pay depended on the results. The effect of this was narrow, boring lessons, not real education. Source 67 describes its faults.

The pressure for more schools eventually could not be resisted. In 1870 an Education Act was passed setting up Board Schools where there were not enough schools already (see Source 68). In the years that followed, school was made compulsory from 5 to 10 and from 1891 it was free.

'Giving education to the working classes would be bad for them. It would teach them to despise their lot in life, instead of making them good workers. Instead of teaching them obedience, it would make them difficult and insolent to their superiors.'

SOURCE 66
Davies Giddy, MP, speaking against educating the poor, 1807 (adapted).

'The great faults of the famous plan of payment by results is that it fosters teaching by rote. It is possible . . . to get children through the examination in reading, writing and [arithmetic] without their really knowing how to read, write or [add up].'

SOURCE 67
Matthew Arnold writing about 'payment by results' in 1869.

SOURCE 68
Nature study lesson in a Board School.

SOURCE 69
Queen Victoria's Diamond Jubilee celebrations, 1897.

The Diamond Jubilee

In 1897 Queen Victoria had been queen for 60 years and there were great celebrations (see Source 69). She appeared as the ruler of a huge, successful Empire. A quarter of the world was hers: 372 million people; 28 million square kilometres. From all over the British Empire, 50,000 troops came to London for the procession. It was the largest procession London had ever seen, from the largest empire the world had ever seen. Behind the Empire was the prosperity and strength of Britain, a leading industrial and commercial nation.

Source 70, however, shows that the clear lead which Britain had once had over all other countries was over. The industrial wealth of Britain, described in this book, was built on trade. By 1900 other countries could compete with Britain on equal, or better, terms. In this situation, building up the Empire was the easy option. It was easier to trade with British possessions overseas, where foreign traders were not welcome. The British share of trade with Europe and North America was falling; trade with the Empire and parts of the world which were like the Empire, such as South America, was rising.

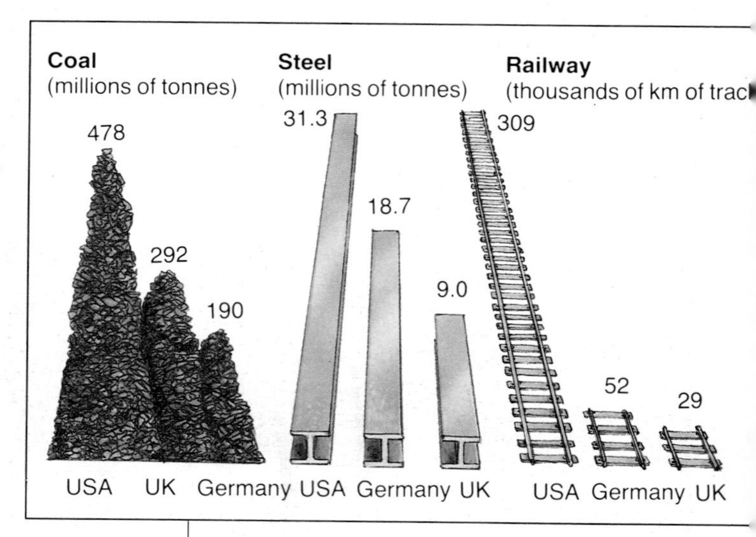

SOURCE 70
Production of coal and steel and railway mileage in the USA, UK and Germany, 1913.

The British people

Source 71 shows some of the British inhabitants of this Empire. Their standard of living was better than it had been 50 years earlier. Full employment and better wages led to better living conditions, improved diet and a healthier lifestyle. People were better educated and now had their own political party, the Labour Party, to speak for them.

However, by any standards, they were still poor. Several of the children in Source 71 have ill-fitting, second-hand clothes and no shoes. Their houses were overcrowded and death from disease was all too common. In 1916, in the Great War, only three out of every nine men called up to serve in the Army were fully fit.

The industrial legacy

The Industrial Revolution described in this book changed the lives of everyone in Britain. The industrialised Britain it created lasted through most of the 20th century. Its legacy is all around us, in factories, mines, ironworks, docks, city halls, and houses.

In the last 20 years, manufacturing industry has declined. Factories and mines have closed. Source 72 shows the last working steam-powered cotton mill. The steam-engine was built in 1894 and once drove 1,090 looms. When the mill closed, only 20 looms were in use. The factory is to become a museum, as a reminder of the period of British expansion, trade and industry.

SOURCE 71
People outside a house in Liverpool, in about 1895.

SOURCE 72
Cotton-spinning machines, Burnley, Lancashire, 1992.

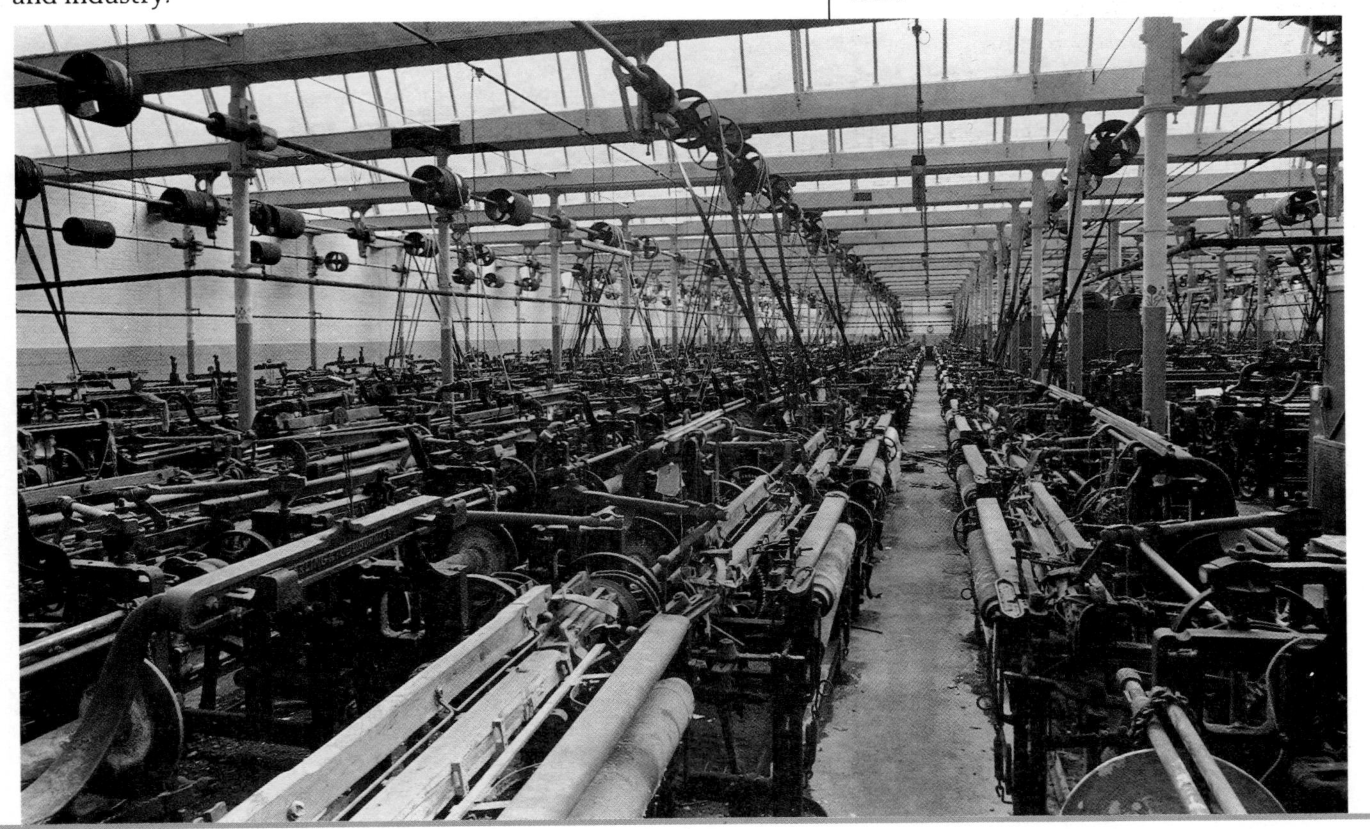

Glossary

Allotment
Small piece of land which people rent to grow crops for their own use, mainly vegetables.

Aqueduct
Bridge carrying a canal.

Bankrupt
Having more debts than money to pay them.

Blast furnace
See *furnace*

Bellows
Machine which pumps a blast of air into a fire or *furnace* to raise the temperature.

Capital
Money put into (*invested* in) a business to get it started or to keep it going. **Capitalist:** someone whose money is invested in this way. If the business does well it pays the capitalist part of the profits, as interest.

Carding
Separating out the strands from the raw wool or cotton before it is spun.

Census
Counting the number of people in the country. A population census has been carried out by the British government every 10 years since 1801 (except for 1941).

Chapel
Where Nonconformists go to worship. Nonconformists are members of religious bodies which are separated from the Church of England, including Baptists and Methodists.

Charcoal
Fuel which produces a lot of heat, made by treating wood.

Clothier
Someone who organised the making of cloth under the *domestic system*, arranging the work of spinners and weavers.

Coke
Fuel made from coal, which produces a greater heat.

Colony
Part of a foreign land settled and ruled by people for the benefit of their own homeland.

Craftspeople
People who make things by using their own skills.

Crop rotation
Changing the crop grown each year on a certain piece of land.

Democracy
System of government where the people choose their rulers by means of voting for them in regular *elections*.

Demonstration
Peaceful protest by marching or making speeches.

Domestic system
The system of making cloth, or any other product, in people's homes.

Dominion
The territory subject to a king or ruler, or under a particular government or control.

Drove road
Wide, green track used to drive animals long distances to market.

Election
Part of a system of *democracy*, in which the people choose from different candidates by voting.

Emigrate
To leave your home country permanently.

Engineering
Designing and making machines.

Entrepreneur
The owner or manager of a business who tries to make profits by trading, involving risks.

Epidemic
Disease affecting a large number of people.

Factory
Building where products are made by machines, usually powered machines.

Fertilising
Adding something to the soil so that it will produce bigger crops.

Fodder
Food for animals.

Forge
Where iron is heated, beaten and shaped.

Freight
Goods in transport.

Furnace
Where iron ore is heated so that the iron becomes liquid and separate.

Glazing
Hard, smooth surface given to pottery.

Horse-power
Way of measuring the strength of power.

Immigration
Moving into a country to live there.

Industrialised
Place or country where *industry* is the most important economic activity.

Industry
Making goods by machine.

Invest
Put money (*capital*) into a business.

Ironfounder
Someone who runs an ironworks.

Justice of the Peace (JP)
Magistrate who is not a lawyer but is given powers to act as a judge in a local court.

Locomotive
Steam engine on wheels which can drive itself.

Magistrate
Official who acts as a judge in law courts which deal with less serious crimes or disputes (see *JPs*).

Malt
Made by roasting barley after it has been soaked; used in making beer.

Manufacturing
Making products for sale.

Millwright
Skilled mechanic, originally working on mills, but using his/her skill to set up and look after factory machinery.

Minister
Person who leads religious worship.

Municipal
To do with towns and cities (see also under *Socialism*).

Mutiny
When soldiers (or sailors) disobey their officers and turn against them.

Nabob
Rich East India Company merchant, living like an Indian prince.

Open field system
System of farming, in use in Britain for many centuries, in which the land was divided into *strips* in large fields, with no dividing hedges. Each villager owned a number of strips in each field and worked the land with everyone else, growing the same crops.

Packhorse
Horse with a large pack on its back, used for transporting goods where wheeled vehicles could not be used.

Paddle-steamer
Steam-powered boat in which the engine drives large, round paddles to make the boat move.

Parson
Parish priest who receives from the people in the parish a tithe (one tenth of their crops or animals each year).

Pawnshop
Shop of a moneylender who lends money in return for goods. You claim your goods back when you can repay the money with interest.

Petition
Signed request from the people to the government.

Pewter
Metal made from 80% tin and 20% lead.

Plantation
System of farming, usually in colonies or ex-colonies, growing a single crop for sale.

Racism
Treatment of some people as inferior because they belong to a particular race.

Radical
Someone who works for a big change in the way the country is governed.

Reform
Change; in particular, changing the way Parliament was elected, who could vote and who could be an MP.

Revolution
Rapid change in a country in which old systems are thrown out and new ones set up.

Rick
A stack or arranged pile of hay or corn.

Rural
In the countryside; the opposite of *urban*.

Settler
Someone who goes to live in a colony.

Sewage
Waste products from people and households.

Shaft
The vertical hole of a pit or mine.

Smallholder
Someone who farms a small piece of land.

Smelting
Obtaining a metal, such as iron, from its ore by heating it in a furnace.

Socialism
Belief that, because the difference between rich and poor is so great, the government should intervene to achieve more equality by helping poor people. 'Municipal Socialism' is where town or city governments raise money by local taxes (rates) and use it to improve conditions.

Spindle
Thin piece of wood on which spun *yarn* was wound.

Squire
The biggest landowner in a village.

Strips
The divisions of land in the *open fields*, usually about 20 metres wide by about 200 metres long.

Subscription
The money paid to join an organisation.

Temperance
Not drinking alcohol.

Terrace
Row of houses, joined together.

Threshing
Separating the grain from the chaff.

Trade union
Organisation of all the workers in a particular trade. They combine together so as to be stronger in pressing for what they each want.

Trading post
Port on the coast where outsiders trade with the people inland.

Transported
Form of punishment in which people were forcibly taken to live and work in a colony, usually Australia.

Urban
To do with towns or cities; opposite of *rural.*

Weaver
The person who makes cloth by weaving the *yarn* on a machine called a loom.

Whig Party
Nineteenth century political group which included people who were eager for political and social reforms.

Yarn
Continuous thread made by spinning fibres of wool or cotton together.

Yeomanry
A cavalry force, formed in 1761, made up of local volunteers.

Index

Page numbers in **bold** refer to illustrations/captions

First published 1993 by CollinsEducational
77-85 Fulham Palace Road
Hammersmith
London W6 8JB

ISBN 0 00 327253 2

Cover design by Glynis Edwards
Book designed by Sally Boothroyd
Series planned by Nicole Lagneau
Edited by Stephen Attmore
Picture research by Celia Dearing
Production by Mandy Inness

Artwork by Linda Rogers Associates/Peter Dennis (on pages 4, 5, 16, 18, 24, 28, 30, 32, 34, 51, 52, 73, 76, 78, 79, 86 and 90) and Angela Lumley (on pages 6, 30, 40, 50 and 66)

Typeset by Dorchester Typesetting Group Ltd, Dorset, UK

Printed and bound in Hong Kong.

Acknowledgements

Photographs The publishers would like to thank the following for permission to reproduce photographs on these pages:

T=top, B=bottom, R=right, C=centre, L=left

Beamish Open Air Museum 7B, 46B, 57, 59; Courtesy Bolton Metro 63TR; Bournville Village Trust 79B; The Bridgeman Art Library/Wallington Hall 3, Manchester City Art Gallery 7T, The British Library 8, London Library 9B, Philip Mould 12, Private Collection 13T, 36T, Clive House Museum 17T, Ironbridge Gorge Museum 26T, Broadlands Trust/Hants 29T, City of Bristol Museum & Art Gallery 31, 36B, RGS 35T, Guildhall Library 38B, Victoria & Albert Museum 41, Iona Antiques 43, 52, Science Museum 47, Royal Holloway & Bedford New College 48, Cheltenham Art Gallery & Museums 50T, 61B, Sheffield Industrial Museum 54T, Christopher Wood Gallery 58T, Courtesy of the Board of Trustees of the V & A 61T, Birmingham City Museums & Art Gallery 76, Guildhall Art Gallery 90; Reproduced by Courtesy of the Trustees of the British Museum 33B; Cambridge University Library 11B; Celtic Picture Library 79T; Chicago Historical Society 33T; Collections/Brian Shuel 17B, 42B, 44; Communist Party Library 74; Courtesy the Cooperative Union Ltd 80B; Crown © Cambridge University Collection of Air Photographs 53L; Cyfarthfa Castle Museum and Art Gallery 18; Robin Dengate 13B; Derby Local Studios Library 11T; Brian Duff 91B; Edifice/Darley 14, 64T; E.T. Archive 39T; Courtesy of the Foreign & Commonwealth Office Library 39B; Courtesy Gladstone Pottery Museum 20, 21B, 61C; John Gorman Collection 81, 83R; Helmshore, Lancashire County Museums 10; David Hey 9T; Holkham Hall 53R; Hulton Deutsch Collection Ltd 27B, 38T, 49C, 56T, 58B, 60T, 62, 87T, 89, 91T; Kelham Island Industrial Museum 19; Courtesy of the Proprietors of the *Lancashire Evening Post*/Lancashire Record Office DDPr 35/23 49T; © Jeremy Lowe, taken from *Welsh Industrial Workers Housing 1775-1875*, Cardiff, (1989) 55; Manchester Central Library 23B, 24, 28, 70; The Mander and Mitchenson Collection 65B; The Mansell Collection 15B, 23T, 25, 37, 42T, 46T, 50B, 56B, 66, 69B, 72, 77, 80T, 83L, 84, 85, 86, 88; D. L. McDougall Collection/The National Waterways Museum 45; Courtesy Lord Middleton 40; The Museum of London 67; The National Museum of Labour History 82; The Board of Trustees of N.M.G.M. 64B/Walker Art Gallery 27T; The National Railway Museum 49B; Collection, Newport Museum and Art Gallery, Gwent 75; O.I.O.C. British Library 35B; Edward Piper 63TL; The Punch Library 58C; Courtesy Rochdale Metro 63B; By permission of the Master and Fellows of St John's College, Cambridge 78; Reproduced by permission of the Trustees of the Science Museum 15T, 29B; The Tate Gallery, London 6; Tolson Museum/Kirklees Metropolitan Council 68; The Victorian Society 60B; Harland Walshaw 54B; Wandsworth Local History Library 65T; Courtesy Wedgwood 21; Welsh Industrial and Maritime Museum 26B; Windsor Castle, Royal Library © 1992 Her Majesty The Queen 71.

Cover photograph: reproduced by kind permission of Lord Romsey, Broadlands Trust